The Davenport Conspiracy

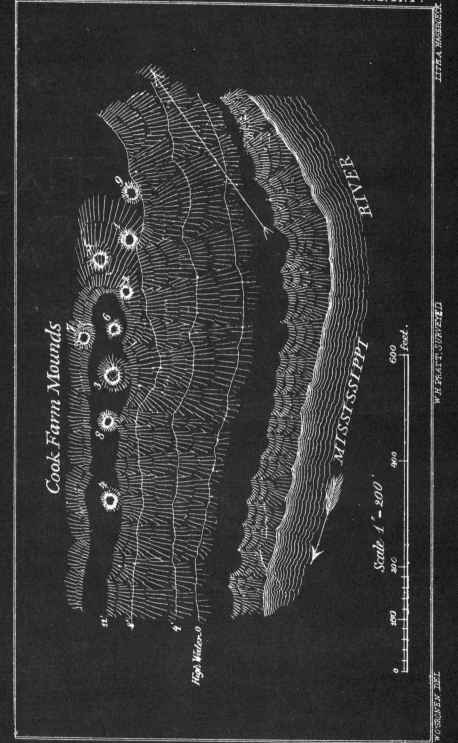

Cook Farm Mounds

MISSISSIPPI RIVER

Scale 1" = 200'

High Water 0

0   100   200   400   600   feet.

LITH.A. HAGEBOECK.

W.H.PRATT, SURVEYED.

WOSGRONEN, DEL.

The Davenport Conspiracy

STATE ARCHAEOLOGIST OF IOWA

Marshall McKusick

Iowa City, Iowa 1970

The Davenport Conspiracy is the first
of a series of reports from the office
of the State Archaeologist, Iowa City.
Other reports will be issued at
intervals.

Copies of this report may be ordered
from the Department of Publications,
The University of Iowa, Iowa City,
Iowa 52240.

Cloth: $5
Paper: $3 (Postage prepaid)

Printed in the United States
of America.

Contents

Plates

Pages 123-142

To Tom Bard Jones

Professor of Ancient History
University of Minnesota

Preface

The discovery of inscribed tablets and elephant pipes
by members of the Davenport Academy developed
into one of the major controversies in the interpretation
of prehistoric America. The private documents bearing
upon this incredible example of nineteenth century
research have never been previously published or even
cited. Full disclosure provides a sordid example of
amateur investigations gone awry during the difficult
transition to professionalism in American archaeology.

A number of people have aided me in the investigation
of the case. Foremost among them was Mr. Donald
Herold, former Director of the Davenport Museum.
He located the original documentation while reorgan-
izing the collections, and I benefited from his discussions on numerous occasions. Mrs. Carol Hunt,
Museum Registrar, was indispensable with documents
and specimens and the present director, Mr. Joseph
Cartwright, allowed copies of all documents to be
placed in The University of Iowa Library, Special
Collections, for future reference. Illustrations were
prepared by The University of Iowa Photographic
Service. Mrs. Jean Young aided me in the writing and
proofreading and during the interviews. Mr. Irving
Hurlbut of Muscatine provided a solution to the
mystery. Mrs. Hertha Gass Erbe of Postville contributed background information about her father, the
Reverend Jacob Gass, discoverer of the specimens
which led to the formation of the Davenport
conspiracy.

Marshall McKusick
State Archaeologist

The Lost Race of Mound Builders

I

Almost a century ago, in eastern Iowa, various groups of mound explorers led by a dedicated amateur archaeologist, the Reverend Jacob Gass, made a most remarkable and significant series of widely publicized discoveries. These finds strongly supported an important archaeological theory generally accepted at the time by many, if not most, antiquarians. Archaeological remains of extensive burial mound groups and other prehistoric earthworks were well known in eastern North America. The various prehistoric peoples who had constructed these earthworks were termed "Mound Builders" in archaeological parlance. The current theory or opinion a century ago held that these ancient mound builders were a lost race, unrelated to the historic tribes of Indians living in North America at the time of European discovery. It was further speculated that the mound builders, believed to be clearly superior in culture to the historic tribes, might even have been prehistoric immigrants from Europe or the Mediterranean high civilizations.

If authentic, the discoveries of the Reverend Mr. Gass and those who worked with him conclusively demonstrated that the mound builders were a lost race—a people with the Old World cultural links. Three inscribed tablets showed beyond question that some of the prehistoric inhabitants of the Midwest wrote in a highly evolved phonetic alphabet related to Hittite or equivalent script. They possessed a calendar, or zodiac, closely duplicating the ancient zodiac long used in the Mediterranean area. Two effigy tobacco pipes, shaped in stone to resemble elephants, proved that the mound builders knew the mastodon. Gass and his fellow mound explorers were widely acclaimed, and the scientific organization sponsoring the work became very well known.

Gass himself modestly declined to interpret his discoveries, leaving such matters to those better qualified. His forte was mound exploration, the recovery of artifacts. Yet such was the obvious importance of the five unique relics to American archaeology that both he and the Davenport Academy inevitably became involved in the subsequent struggles over the question of authenticity.

1

The Davenport Academy

The excavations leading to the discovery of elephant pipes and inscribed tablets had been sponsored by the Davenport Academy of Science as part of a general program to develop knowledge of local flora, fauna, geology, and archaeology. The establishment of local scientific societies was a phenomenon characteristic of the nineteenth century, and the Davenport Academy ranked among the most successful of the private organizations of its type in the country. At the outset of the controversy described in this book, it was assembling large and valuable research collections, and had established a respected publication series.

In his article on the early history of the Davenport Academy, Professor Frederick Starr (1897a) describes a small dedicated group of amateur scientists who began meeting in the year 1867. They collected all manner of things: rocks, minerals, artifacts, shells, and plants. We may suspect their wives frequently encouraged them to move their private collections elsewhere, and before long the group established a museum (plate 18). As interest in their projects grew, they published compilations of brief descriptive notes in volumes entitled the *Proceedings of the Davenport Academy of Natural Sciences*. The Academy was an association of local men with an interest in natural history; in today's idiom, one main purpose was "adult education." Professional scientists living outside the Davenport area were corresponding members who aided the group with counsel, talks, and who often published articles in the *Proceedings*.

Local scientific academies were not uncommon at this time in the state. Groups similar to the one in Davenport met in Sioux City and Muscatine, and probably other cities as well. Some members of each were actively pursuing the study of prehistoric archaeology, and preliminary reports briefly noted the findings. In Iowa City, on a more professional level, a group of professors at the University organized the Iowa Academy of Science. It developed into a state-wide group, the last survivor in name of the various academies formed during this period. The decline and disappearance of the local groups was in part due to limited membership. No single city possessed the intellectual and financial resources to carry out the ambitious research plans in various fields envisioned by the founders of these academies.

To explain the growth of scientific clubs and societies, not only in Iowa but throughout the country, it may be pointed out that it was an era of pre-professionalism in science. Full-time research specialists were rare, and the learned publications representing some fields could probably be read in a few months. Amateurs could and did make contributions, if not to theory, at least to gathering basic data which could lead to interpretations by those more fully trained and sophisticated. During this time the Davenport Academy members—a small group, a handful, who actually did field work and presented papers at the meetings—collected information in a number of fields. In the next generation, when science became more complex and more exacting, the various local academies became extinct. It was no accident. The best of the amateurs became professionals or dropped out, and the academies became museums dedicated to public information and education rather than undertaking research. The regional universities, as learned institutions, were assuming intellectual dominance. At the time we are describing, however, these trends in American life were not yet generally evident.

The Mastodon Question

During the second half of the nineteenth century one of the major archaeological questions was the contemporaneity of man and mastodon in North America. To almost all of the investigators who looked into the matter, there seemed little reason to doubt various reports of a general association of some artifacts with the bones of extinct elephants. Otis T. Mason (1880b:815) remarked in the *American Naturalist,* "It is as yet an open question whether man existed on this continent contemporaneously with the mastodon, or, what amounts to the same thing, whether the mastodon survived until man had appeared in America." It did not, in fact, amount to the "same thing" for some thought man might be very ancient in America—even pre-glacial in age. Sources of these reports appear in Farquharson (1877), Charles E. Putnam's *Elephant Pipes . . .* (1886) and others. In a series of articles and editorials in the *American Antiquarian,* Stephen Peet argued that the mastodon extinction was recent, citing a number of excavation reports suggesting recent deposition and excellent preservation of the fossils. The evidence provided the subject of Chapter Three, "The Mound Builders and the Mastodon" which appeared in Peet's book, *The Mound Builders: their Works and Relics* (2nd ed. 1903).

Shortly thereafter this point of view was modified. In 1907, the eminent physical anthropologist, Ales Hrdlicka, published the classic study, "Skeletal Remains Suggesting or Attributed to Early Man in North America" showing the inadequacies of the human skeletal evidence for man's antiquity. He produced such effective arguments in a series of later studies that the question was not seriously reopened until the late 1920s when Figgins, a paleontologist associated with the Denver Museum of Natural History, found Folsom points and an extinct form of bison clearly associated together in New Mexico. Others found Clovis points and mammoth during the 1930s, and current opinions on early man are discussed at length by Willey (1966: 26-77) and Jennings (1968:39-108). These later shifts in interpretation and findings, however, are irrelevant here. At the time of the Davenport discoveries in the 1870s, men acquainted with contemporary archaeological reports anticipated finding evidence of men with the mastodon. Indeed, if such evidence came to light locally, it would be an important buttress of widespread speculation and would be certain to draw attention to the scientific program of the Academy.

Who Were the Mound Builders?

A second archaeological problem argued and discussed at great length concerned the identification of the "Mound Builders." One of the major intellectual contributions to American archaeology appeared in the *Second Annual Report* of the U.S. Bureau of Ethnology published in 1883, and culminated in the *Twelfth Annual Report* of 1894. Under the leadership of Major John W. Powell, the group of scholars associated with the bureau began to refute the mass of contradictory, confused, and unfounded speculations about the mysterious mound builders. They began a systematic program establishing the Indian continuities in the North American archaeological sequence, demonstrating the falsity of lost races and other farfetched explanations for the origins of the widespread and elaborate prehistoric earthworks.

Various mound builder theories current before the nineteenth century became more elaborate with the beginning of archaeological surveys. These are discussed by Douglas W. Schwartz (1967:6-31) with reference to the development of Kentucky archaeology, but his description is more generally applicable to the Mississippi Valley. A common early view that long persisted considered the unsettled historic Indians to be preceded by culturally superior civilized men. Some scholars, notably Samuel F. Haven (1855), argued that indigenous Indians built the mounds, an unpopular concept running counter to the racist belief that only "white Indians" possessed the ability to make such elaborate earthworks. The arguments of a   lost race were hard to quell. The landmark report in American archaeology by E. G. Squier and E. H. Davis (1848) "Ancient Monuments of the Mississippi Valley . . ." took the view that there were two distinct cultures—Indian and Mound Builder. They concluded that the mound builders were probably of Mexican origin or possibly that the mound builders moved from the Mississippi Valley into Mexico itself (Schwartz 1967:20). This report was repeatedly cited to reinforce the belief that local Indians did not make the earlier mounds.

In the early Iowa reports on archaeological discoveries, the division between mound builders and Indians was taken for granted and colored the interpretations of the evidence. A few examples suggest the local views. Samuel Murdock from Elkader published an article about his excavations in the *Iowa Historical Record* saying:

> Not until the Indian had glided out of sight did we begin to suspect that he himself was but the successor of other and distinct races who had preceded him. . . . It is now generally conceded that the "Mound-builder" was distinct and separate from all other races of the globe; that the race is now, and has been for centuries, totally extinct. (1888:28, 30).

Samuel Calvin, an early State Geologist of Iowa, presented a commonly held view of the place of the mound builders. In his public address on this popular topic published in the series *Iowa Historical Lectures*, Calvin (1893) described the sequence of three distinct races: a low-browed Neanderthal type, succeeded first by the mound builders, and finally by the Indian race. He left open the question of the genetic relationship of these races. Some theories die slowly. It may be of passing interest to note that Thomas Christensen, as late as 1952, considered it important to scotch the belief about the local mounds. In the *Annals of Iowa*, he published an article discussing the reasons why ". . . there was no mysterious *general race* of Mound Builders, distinct from the historic tribes." (1952:300).

At the time of the Davenport Academy explorations in the 1870s, the mound builder thesis was widely accepted, and continued with surprising viability thereafter. Five unique artifacts, found by members under auspicious circumstances with witnesses, demonstrated that the two current themes of archaeology—elephants and lost race—were related to the local prehistoric earthworks.

If Accepted as Credible

Cyrus Thomas, Director of Archaeology at the U.S. Bureau of Ethnology in Washington, was to struggle with the Davenport controversy in his publications for over a decade. His extensive monograph of 1894 on mound explorations contained a lengthy section on various theories. In reviewing and discarding faulty evidence, Thomas was forced to dismiss as invalid the Davenport artifacts, as he had previously done in an earlier series of papers.

> If the marks upon these tablets are true letters or alphabetic signs, and are the work of the veritable mound-builders, it must be admitted that those who made them were not Indians but a people much further advanced in the arts of civilized life than most of the known aborigines of the continent. . . . The theory that the mounds were the work of a lost race of comparatively civilized people who occupied this country in the far distant past, had taken hold of a large portion of our archaeologists. There have long been a hope and belief that at some time discoveries would be made to confirm this. It was also further believed that the mammoth or American elephant was still in existence when this civilized race inhabited the country, but satisfactory evidence on these points was wanting.
>
> The objects and uses of the so-called "altars" found chiefly in the Ohio mounds were unsettled questions.
>
> Suddenly the archaeological world is surprised at finding itself in possession of proof on all these points. A tablet is taken from a mound under the very shadow of one of our leading scientific academies on which is an inscription of sufficient length to silence all doubt as to its being alphabetic, and immediately under it is the altar with the smoking sacrifice or burning body on it. Nay, more, on the reverse is the figure of the elephant. Nor is this all: In the same mound is another tablet with markings for the zodiacal signs, a calendar in fact. But good fortune, not satisfied with this generosity, throws into the hands of the same individual two elephant pipes, so distinct that there can be no doubt as to the animal intended. To clinch this evidence and show that it relates to the true mound-builders, the fairy goddess leads the same hands to a mound which contains a tablet bearing figures of the veritable mound-builders' pipes and copper axe, some of the letters on the the other tablet and the sun symbol. Thanks to the energy of one person the evidence on all these questions is furnished, which, if accepted as credible, must forever settle them. (Thomas 1894:632-633, 642).

The question, however, hung on the phrase "if accepted as credible." The Davenport discoveries accepted by many scholars for a decade or longer represented one of the most bitterly contested hoaxes in American archaeology.

A recently published book, *Mound Builders of Ancient America: the Archaeology of a Myth,* is an interesting and excellent review of the clash of theories and the solution of the mound builder question in American archaeology. The author, Robert Silverberg (1968), discusses the Davenport discoveries in some detail, relying on the published attack by Henry W. Henshaw (1883), the first edition of the fierce and lengthy defense by Charles E. Putnam (1885), and the final summation and rejection of the artifacts by Cyrus Thomas (1894) of the U.S. Bureau of Ethnology. There is considerably more to the Davenport controversy than Silverberg suggests, but much of the story has been hidden away in manuscript files at the Davenport Musuem and in the memories of a few elderly Iowans.

Discovery of the Five Unique Relics

2

The Reverend Jacob Gass, discoverer of the unique Davenport artifacts, was born in 1842 in Oltingen and studied theology in Basel. While still a young man in 1868, he emigrated from Switzerland to the United States, continuing his theological training at Wartburg Seminary, then located in Strawberry Point, Iowa. Ordained in 1871, he began his career at the First Lutheran Zion Church in Davenport (Gass Erbe 1969MS). This background would be irrelevant, except that Davenport had a very large German and German-speaking population. The Reverend Mr. Gass preached and taught in German and was not yet fluent in English—at least, he could not write it, and this would prove a handicap. More important, the New England Yankees and the German-speaking immigrants were often figuratively, as well as literally, not on the best of speaking terms.

He became interested in local archaeology. In 1874 with the help of his brother-in-law, A. Borgelt, and two other theological students, he excavated a series of prominent burial mounds on the Cook Farm. The site, then located on the outskirts of Davenport, is now near the center of town, and covered with a factory. The mound explorations uncovered a remarkable series of genuine, and for Iowa, unprecedented artifacts.

Cook Farm Excavations

The artifacts excavated at the Cook Farm would now be grouped within the Hopewellian tradition and represent burial cult objects of great rarity. A number of green and grey pipestone pipes were found. The material, if not the finished pipes themselves, is typical of Hopewellian pipes found in Ohio (Shetrone 1930MSa). Some of these platform pipes were beautifully shaped to resemble animals including a frog, a bird, and a doglike effigy (plate 11). The plain platform pipes (plate 13.1, 3, 4, 5) were perfectly proportioned and finished. Subsequent studies by Shetrone (1930MS, 1930MSa) and by the author have confirmed the genuineness of these specimens, although the frog pipe has been questioned by Griffin (1965:160) on what we believe to be insufficient grounds.

In addition to the pipes, Gass recovered Hopewell pottery and superb examples of flint implements and other artifacts. What attracted the most attention at the time was a series of native copper axes. These had been originally placed in individual cloth bags, and the textile fabric was partially preserved by the contact with the copper itself. Elaborate burial rituals were indicated by the presence of stone groupings termed "altars," stone slabs laid over the burial areas, and layers of shell and ash in the mounds. Some of the burials were extended, that is, laid out in the horizontal position, and others were flexed in what appeared to the investigators to be sitting positions. The total assemblages, including obsidian and marine shell, ceramics, pipes and bone artifacts, fit within the classic Hopewellian tradition, and in terms of modern radiocarbon chronology date within a range from about 300 B.C. to A.D. 300. It should be emphasized, however, that this variety of Hopewellian artifacts is extremely rare in Iowa. The ceramics appear in mounds along the bluffs of the Mississippi and sporadically inland as far as Boone, above Des Moines, on the Des Moines River (see McKusick 1964:99-100). Platform pipes rarely occur in Iowa. Several have been found in mounds along the Upper Iowa River in northeast Iowa, and a single example has been reported from Webster County in central Iowa. All other examples known to me come from a restricted area of southeast Iowa, from large mounds on the Mississippi bluffs between Davenport and Burlington. The fortuitous discovery of such finds led Gass to increase the scope of his activity.

The first reports of the Cook Farm discoveries were published by the Reverend Mr. Gass in the local German newspapers. As word reached the English-speaking community, a prominent member of the Davenport Academy became most interested. Dr. Robert J. Farquharson was a local physician. He published a description of the excavations and specimens in 1875 in the *Proceedings of the American Association for the Advancement of Science,* and substantially the same article appeared in the Davenport Academy *Proceedings* in 1876. The description of the excavations was based upon personal observations and newspaper accounts, and an Academy colleague, W. H. Pratt, illustrated the article with diagrams and information supplied by Gass. Dr. Farquharson encouraged Gass to join the Academy and conduct his explorations on behalf of that organization. The admission of an outsider to the Academy did not sit well with some of the other members, an inference drawn from the Judge James Wills Bollinger narrative of the affair as told to Irving Hurlbut (1969MS). For a

number of years, members had dug into mounds on both sides of the
Mississippi River without obtaining much in the way of results. Now
an energetic, young, and dedicated Swiss was finding treasures of
antiquity near Davenport itself. Although he did not speak English
fluently, we may suppose he made his point that systematic work
rather than random excursions provided results. Some of the members
considered Gass to be a "windjammer and liar," which led to hard
feeling about his archaeological successes (Hurlbut 1969MS).

Discovery of the Slate Tablets

In January 1877, the indefatigable minister returned to the Cook
Farm mounds to complete his 1874 excavation of Mound 3. The largest
of the Cook Farm mound group, it measured fifty-five feet across and
seven feet high. Previously, Gass had shoveled through two historic
Indian burials with European trade goods in oak "coffins." Beneath
these intrusive burials, he had discovered earlier skeletons with five
prehistoric copper axes wrapped in cloth, two pipes, one of them
resembling a groundhog or dog, and a number of other objects.

The clergyman now began a salvage excavation in the middle of an
Iowa winter. This was necessary because a new tenant was soon taking
over the lease of the Cook Farm. The minister and his friends would
not be allowed to dig on the farm later in the year. Rather than allow
any part of the mound to remain for other relic hunters, Gass decided
to finish it himself, regardless of difficulties. Gass was assisted by
seven German friends, who smashed through the upper two and one-
half feet of the frozen ground and poked a hole into the remnant of
the mound. They first encountered another historic Indian burial, *with
the bones scattered and disturbed,* and they picked up some glass
beads and part of a brass ring before plunging their hole more deeply,
going through two layers of shells. They uncovered a burial pit with
loose black soil containing some human bone fragments and slate
fragments. Here the human bones were also in disorder, unlike the
complete skeletons from the adjacent burial area excavated in Mound
3 in 1874 (plate 15).

> These circumstances arrested particular attention, and caused me
> to proceed with more caution, until soon after,—about five o'clock
> in the afternoon,—we discovered the two inscribed tablets of coal
> slate. . . . The smaller one is engraved on one side only, and the
> larger on both sides. The larger one was lying with that side up-
> ward which was somewhat injured by a stroke with the spade. . . .

> Both were closely encircled by a single row of limestones. They
> were closely encircled by a single row of limestones. They were
> covered on both sides with clay, on removal of which the markings
> were for the first time discovered. . . . It should also be remarked
> that I did not leave the mound after penetrating through the frost
> until the tablets were discovered and taken from their resting place
> with my own hands. (Gass 1877a:96).

The entire excavation, including breaking the frozen ground, was ac-
complished most hastily, and took only a single winter day. In his
1877 report, Gass corrects some of the earlier statements made by
Farquharson in the publications of 1875 and 1876. Mound 3 was 10
feet more in diameter (65 feet) and only 3 or 4 feet high (instead of
7). The stratigraphy is explained in more detail and the oak coffins
of the historic Indians are now described as oak boughs. These corrections of the 1874 excavation are "from notes taken at the time."
(Gass 1877a:93). It may be noted that "coal slate" is actually a form
of shale obtainable locally. The report by Gass was written in German
and translated into English for the Academy.

The smaller tablet, appropriately named the Calendar stone, was inscribed with four concentric circles around a central dot or pit, crudely
scribed, yet suggestive of the use of a drawing compass (plate 3). The
circles were ornamented with marks designating the four cardinal di-
rections and were interspersed with zodiac-appearing symbols; all
were distinctly non-Indian. The larger slab, named the Hunting Scene
tablet, was covered on one side with crude outline drawings of men
and animals. One of these animals was drawn with a large snout suggesting it was intended to portray an elephant or tapir (plate 2). The
other side, usually referred to as the Cremation Scene, depicted a
group of Indians holding hands and grouped around a mound which
had a sacrificial fire blazing on top; above the mound were representations of the sun, moon, and stars; the upper portion of the tablet bore
a lengthy and curious inscription which could not be deciphered
(plate 1). The Academy recorded in the *Proceedings* a vote of thanks
to Mr. Gass "for his interesting paper, for the zeal and intelligence with
which he has prosecuted his successful archaeological researches . . ."
(PDANS 2:82).

Because of the unprecedented discovery, it was thought desirable to
append "certificates" from the various participants confirming and
substantiating the account of the discoveries written by Gass. The 1874
excavation account was certified by three men including a brother-in-

law named A. Borgelt. The more remarkable finds of 1877 were supported by the signatures of seven other men. Not one of these men belonged to the Davenport Academy at the time the tablets were discovered and only one would later be elected to membership. They were all Germans and several were clergy. The excavation of 1877 seems to have included another brother-in-law of Gass named Adolf Blumer. It may be coincidental, but Blumer was later to discover the elephant pipe.

The Limestone Tablet

The Cook Farm, then situated on the outskirts of Davenport, held other surprises. A year later, in January 1878, Gass gained permission to dig, and with two hardy friends, John Hume and Charles E. Harrison, extended the domain of science by carefully smashing up burial Mound 11 which was frozen to a depth of seven or eight inches. His two friends were also members of the Academy and according to Putnam (1886:261) both "well and favorably known in this community."

Success rewarded their enterprise: they found a magnificently painted and "inscribed" tablet (plate 4) in a chamber built up of stones. When the ten pieces were reassembled, the limestone tablet portrayed an Indian and two effigy pipes.

> The circumstances of this discovery, as narrated by Mr. Harrison, are published in the Proceedings of the Academy [PDANS 2:221-224]. No suspicions whatever attach to this discovery, and the well-attested facts connected therewith establish, beyond reasonable doubt, that, whether more or less ancient, the tablet was deposited at the making of the mound. (Putnam 1886:261).

Elephant Pipes

The two elephant pipes (plate 5.1, 2) resembled in their general configuration animal platform pipes sometimes found in midwestern mounds. The circumstances of recovery seemed beyond doubt, considering frequently worse documented finds characteristic of this period.

During an archaeological exploring trip to Louisa County, south of Davenport, Gass heard about an unusual pipe owned by a farmer. Following up this story, he saw the pipe, recognized the importance of the carved elephant, and borrowed it to have casts and photographs made at the Davenport Academy, since the farmer refused to sell this remarkable object. During casting, the original was accidentally dropped and broken in half. In order to appease the owner, the Academy paid a small sum and purchased the elephant pipe, since repairs had rendered it worthless for smoking. A totally inconsequential observation may be introduced to illustrate the vagueness which surrounded the purchase of this unique specimen. The curator, W. H. Pratt, reports the amount paid was about five dollars (PDANS 2:349), as does Farquharson (1880:67) in the *American Antiquarian.* On the other hand, Barber (1882:276), in an article on mound pipes, reports the sum was three or four dollars as does a subsequent director, John Bailey (1948:3-4).

The published account of the history of the find, written before the controversy, states that a German farmer, Peter Mare, found the pipe in a cornfield, and the catalogue entry gives the date of this find as March 1873. He attached no particular importance to the object and sometimes smoked it. Upon leaving for Kansas, Mare gave it to his brother-in-law who was the owner when Gass obtained it for the Academy (PDANS 2:349, note).

In 1880, the Reverend Adolf Blumer, a Lutheran minister from Geneseo, Illinois, excavated a mound on the farm of Peter Haas in Louisa County. The excavation report by Blumer (1882) describes the upper layer of the mound as hard clay, some eighteen inches thick, with some indications of fire action. Underlying this was a layer of red colored, hard burned clay. This second layer was a lens, three feet thick in the center tapering to three inches thick around the edges. In size, the lens was about five feet across the shorter diameter. The third layer was a lens of ash, thirteen inches thick at the center and diminishing towards the edges. In these ashes, the excavators found part of a bird pipe and a small copper axe; Blumer himself removed the celebrated elephant pipe. It may be noted that he was aided in his excavation by several neighboring farmers, the son of the landowner, and his brother-in-law, who was none other than Gass.

Embarrassed With its Richness

Although some doubts about the inscribed tablets were locally current at the time of discovery, they were largely laid to rest by the appearance of affidavits, called "certificates," from the explorer-excavators (see Gass 1877a:98). Dr. Farquharson, elected president of the

Academy the next year, addressed the membership on the importance of the discovery:

> We are, in a measure, astonished at the unexpectedness of our discovery, and also somewhat embarrassed with its richness; for in one particular, (that of phonetic writing), it seems to prove too much. . . . It is objected, and seriously, too, that this discovery comes too *apropos,* too pat, in fact, and so partakes in the minds of some too much of the nature of a stage trick, a *Deus ex Machina.* However, if it is a true, *bona fide* discovery, some one else among the great army of searchers, in the course of time and from the very necessity of the case, must have made the same or a like one. . . . However, whether by fortune or misfortune, it has been our lot to make the discovery, and it now becomes our duty, honestly and firmly convinced as we are, of its genuineness and authenticity, fairly to publish it to the scientific world, for its merits there to be adjudged, inviting all fair and candid criticism. (Farquharson 1877:103).

He was well aware of the controversy which such a find would bring, in particular the side of the tablet with the inscription:

> Here, as well as anywhere, I may mention that one great objection to the reception of this or any other discovery of an inscription, seeming to come from the mounds, arises from the fact that most writers on American antiquities of any authority, however much they may differ on other matters, seem as one on this point, that no American race ever had a written phonetic language; some even go further, and say that as no evidence of such has been found, none ever will be found. (Ibid., 104).

Continuing with discretion, he reviewed the history of ten reported inscriptions "both true and false" including Dighton Rock; the Grave Creek Stone; the Nova Scotia, Ohio, and Pemberton (New Jersey) axes; the Holy Stones of Wyrick, and others, mentioning the doubts and controversies. After these cautions, Farquharson notes that when one looks at the Davenport tablets with a magnifying glass the incisions are uniform and nowhere deep; the original marks of smoothing and polishing are present on the surface, indicating the stone "had not weathered much." His discussion of the Calendar stone points out an interesting aspect of the dimensions. It is seven inches square, with two suspension holes three-eighths of an inch in diameter. One side is plain, the other inscribed. The inner circle has a diameter of two inches and three outer concentric circles are each separated by spacing nearly three-quarters of an inch.

> This certainly has a modern look, but the apparent agreement with modern measures of length may be, after all, merely a coincidence. . . . If we consider this a calendar stone, and the twelve (12) signs as marking the divisions of the year, then it does not in the least resemble the Mexican and Maya calendars. If again we consider it as zodiacal, the signs in the outer circle being symbols of the constellations along the sun's path, then, though the signs are different, yet the resemblance to the common zodiac is so great as to suggest contact with one of the many nations or races which have adopted that very ancient delineation of the sun's pathway through the heavens. (Ibid., 109).

The second slate tablet had split along a plane of cleavage so that the two sides were separate. The most interesting side, broken in half by the shovel, portrayed a "sacrificial or cremation scene" with an Indian mound ceremony surmounted by an inscription in letters or hieroglyphics. Earlier in the paper he had offhandedly remarked ". . . finding the letters *T, O, W, N,* in the Davenport inscription 'may be' pure fancy." (Ibid., 107). The unbroken, but separate underside of the tablet is referred to as the Hunting Scene; it had 30 figures which he identified as 8 men, 4 bison, 4 deer, 3 birds, 3 hares, and single examples of a big horn or Rocky Mountain goat, a fish, and a prairie wolf. Finally, there were 3 nondescript animals which could represent she-moose, tapirs, or mastodon. Farquharson favored the mastodon identification and reviewed reports purporting to show its recent extinction in North America. He concluded that the chain of evidence was complete, linking the mound builder with written language, Old World culture, and elephants.

Trappers, Knaves, and Mormons

3

The Davenport Academy acted swiftly and with the greatest propriety. The Reverend Jacob Gass discovered the unique slate tablets in January 1877, and the following April, encased in plaster and wooden frames, they arrived at the Smithsonian. The Secretary of the Institution, Professor Spencer Baird, wrote to the Academy, "There appears every indication of genuineness in the specimens, and the discovery is certainly one of very high interest." (cited by Putnam 1886:342). Photographs were taken and "duplicates" exhibited informally to members of the National Academy of Sciences meeting in Washington. In May 1877, Baird again wrote to Davenport. "An official presentation was prevented by the press of other business that pressed it out of place. Most of the persons who examined them—among whom were Professor Haldeman, Mr. Lewis H[enry] Morgan, and others—were of the opinion that they were unquestionably of great antiquity. . . . Most of them, however, preferred to defer any formal consideration of the subject." (Ibid., 343).

In May, Dr. E. Foreman wrote to J. Duncan Putnam giving his informal conclusion. The letter reads in part, "Prof. Baird has requested me to make a report upon [the tablets]—and as he gave me to understand that great antiquity has been ascribed to these works, it may be proper to say to you that I am unable to coincide in the opinion and shall have to report against it." (Foreman 1877MS). The report itself was soon finished and a copy was forwarded to the Academy where it aroused considerable anger. It survives today as a nine-page, handwritten document on legal size paper. Never published by the Smithsonian, parts of this report are of interest, for the questions raised by Foreman (1877MSa) were to survive in the later struggles over the authenticity.

Thoroughly Ransacked

In his manuscript, Foreman reviews the excavation and finds from Cook Farm Mound 3 in detail, for he had access to the Gass report (1877a:96), at that time still in manuscript, but translated into English. The map plan of the burials (plate 15), he emphasized as a significant part of the interpretation. In 1874, Gass excavated burial pit

A, finding the skeletons intact and undisturbed. The excavation in 1877 of burial pit *B* encountered thoroughly scattered and incomplete skeletons with the slate tablets. Foreman suspected that burial pit *B* had been "thoroughly ransacked," explaining why the excavator, Gass, could not decide how many individuals had been interred or what the original burial position had been.

> He found no entire skeleton in its proper place. The other grave had yielded some copper axes and other relics usually buried with their owners but this one contained only a "bit of copper" which, after being in contact with some bones a long time and saturating them with the green carbonate, was discovered lying at a distance from them. By referring to the decent order in which the grave *A* was found and using it as a term of comparison with *B*, it must be concluded that both graves were constructed at the same time and in a similar manner, and in due turn both were occupied by deceased persons, that one of them had been undisturbed until Mr. Gass' explorations, and the other, as may be deduced from his own statements, had been previously entered and its entire contents thrown into confusion, at which time it may also be inferred, that the tablets he discovered had been introduced for the purpose of deception. That the layers of shells of this part of the mound were found apparently in their original place cannot be regarded as absolute proof that the mound was for the first time opened by Mr. Gass since a person engaged in practising such a deception would cover up any traces of his work by replacing so conspicuous an object, as he had found it. (Foreman 1877MSa.)

Interpreting the Inscriptions

Having established the apparently disturbed archaeological context of burial pit *B*, Foreman attempted to interpret the meaning of the inscriptions. After describing the Cremation Scene tablet (plate 1) he wrote:

> In this picture the artist would seem to have endeavored to depict his religious creed, or points of belief relative to the passage of the disembodied spirit of an Indian from its terrestrial surroundings, through a place of probation to its final reception in the place of departed spirits, commonly spoken of as the happy hunting grounds. The spaces enclosed by the arched lines, are conjectured to mean the place of probation or purgatory, as taught by the Roman Catholic church, which intercepts the passing spirit, that the sins committed during his life may be expiated and any taint of worldly grossness cleansed away. The absence of any thing like human figures in these spaces may be accounted for upon the belief that the departed spirit is divested of all fleshly covering and therefore becomes in-

visible. The other accessories consisting of figures approaching the forms of circles, squares, ellipses with some of serpentine form may be tortured into meaning almost any thing. (Foreman 1877MSa).

Similarly, he regarded the Hunting Scene tablet (plate 2) as conveying the same general meaning. The tree and the animals represent terrestrial surroundings abandoned by the Indian upon his death. The spirit arises to the hunting grounds represented upon the upper portion of the tablet and is blocked by a barrier.

> The whole is therefore interpreted to mean that the spirit upon leaving its earthly habiliments rises to the barrier interposed in front of the celestial space and comes face to face with the inexorable judge. This is all inconsistent with our received notions of Indian superstitions. The warrior leads such a life, as he thinks should give him a title to enter unquestioned into the land of spirits. His skill in hunting, his contempt for danger in battle, for bodily pain, for death itself—are his passports—not forgetting the treaties broken, scalps taken and horses stolen, are virtuous actions standing to his credit. An Egyptian believed this inquisitional function was performed by Osiris, the Greeks and Romans had their Minos and Rhadamanthus, and in his Vision of Judgement Lord Byron has the line, "Saint Peter sat by the celestial gate" which may stand for the religious creed of Western Europe, but we are not apprised that the Indian mythology includes a functionary clothed with similar attributes. (Foreman 1877MSa).

The Calendar tablet (plate 3) was obviously the zodiac

> . . . commonly seen in almanacs. By forcing the imagination a crab, scorpion, bow and arrow, and the twins may be made out. . . . As the Indians generally divide the revolving year into thirteen nearly equal periods, corresponding to the lunar periods, it must be evident that the tablet does not exhibit Indian ideas but those of the pale face. The fresh appearance of the incisions on this tablet and the exactness with which they may be imitated by the revolving point of a sharp steel instrument, suggest this plate to be even more recent than the others. The circles were probably made by revolving the sharp point of steel compasses used by carpenters in laying off their work. (Foreman 1877MSa).

Indian Convert, Half Breed, or Trapper

> The date of these works may be inferred from the character of the ideas portrayed on them. They set forth the teaching of the Missionary fathers of the Catholic church and the date of their fabrication, must be limited to the time when these courageous and self-sacrificing men are supposed to have penetrated from Montreal or Quebec, through the Lakes to the Mississippi River. This event is

usually stated to have occurred about two hundred and thirty years ago. We are reduced to the belief that these tablets were engraved at some mission house or trading post established by Europeans on the upper Mississippi since A.D. 1640; probably by an Indian convert, a half breed or possibly a Canadian trapper, who were lounging away a long cold winter at a frontier settlement waiting for the season to open for setting their traps for Beaver. The date cannot be rated older than this and may be brought down a hundred or a hundred and fifty years, to comparatively modern times. (Foreman 1877MSa).

An Act of Knavery?

The manuscript report ends, but there is a postscript in the same handwriting suggesting an entirely different origin than the manufacture by a convert or trapper influenced by the good Catholic fathers. It reads:

> The engraving of the tablets is not incompatible with the belief that they were at first a harmless pastime, the Knavery commences with the introduction of them into a mound centuries old for the purpose of deception. Nor is it probable that an Indian would undertake this part of the performance since there are but few more powerful superstitions among the tribes than their abhorrence for disturbing the bones of their fathers. (Foreman 1877MSa).

Such a conclusion, suggesting an act of "knavery" and no antiquity for the tablets, did not sit easily with two principals of the Academy. Mr. W. H. Pratt, the owner of the Davenport Commercial College, was one of the leading members, serving continuously in one office or another since the Academy began in 1867. Pratt's real interest was natural history; after election to a term as president in 1880-1881, he gave up business entirely to dedicate himself exclusively as the first full-time, paid curator through what would prove to be the coming crisis. His most promising and interested student was J. Duncan Putnam, eldest son of a wealthy lawyer and businessman. Duncan Putnam's primary interest was entomology, and he attended Harvard intermittently, as his delicate health would allow. Upon the death of the younger Putnam at the early age of 26 in 1881, his father, Charles E. Putnam, absorbed himself in the Academy proving himself the champion of the relics which his favorite son had defended in the last years of his life. Pratt and Duncan Putnam were close friends despite the great disparity in age of almost thirty years, and Duncan Putnam bought Pratt a life membership in the Academy, which suggests that the management of the Commercial College had been somewhat neglected for science. In the spring of 1877, Duncan Putnam and Pratt consulted by memoranda with each other (Foreman 1877MS), and decided that a vigorous reply to Foreman and his report was in order. They sent off letters of criticism which are not preserved in copy, but the replies to their letters and their marks on Foreman's manuscript clearly suggest the line of defense. They disputed the ransacked, disturbed appearance of grave *B*, the extent of copper stains on the child burial, cited Foreman's failure to list other artifacts from grave *B*, denied that the shell strata above the burials had been replaced, and were able to state positively that the two inner surfaces of the large tablet did not have inscriptions prior to being covered with the plaster used in mounting them. They objected additionally to the interpretation of the cremation scene as Catholic inspired, denied a steel tool could have been used—or a carpenter's compass for that matter—disputed that the hunting scene was made by a different hand from the cremation scene, and corrected the statement that four marks were scratched on each quadrant of the calendar tablet, because in fact, only three appear. Foreman replied to Duncan Putnam on 22 June, reaffirming his position by saying the tablets were "fishy," and answered some of this barrage of criticism. "Speculations are always assailable and seldom carry with them the force of an argument. I do not advise you therefore to print my report, whilst at the same time I have seen no reason whatever to change my views of this subject." (Ibid.)

Baird Indulges in Public Relations

While Foreman defended his objections to the tablets, Spencer Baird thought matters had gone too far and repudiated Foreman's report. He apparently accepted the judgment of Duncan Putnam and Pratt that Foreman had been hasty and inaccurate. On the same day that Foreman wrote Putnam that Baird supported him, Baird himself wrote that he did not. Such divergence in viewpoint at the Smithsonian must have made Duncan Putnam laugh for he probably received both letters at about the same time. Baird wrote:

> The criticisms of Dr. Foreman on the tablets are not to be considered of any weight whatever nor as expressing any views which the Smithsonian Institution may be supposed to entertain in regard to them. I do not believe he has read, or at least very carefully, the full history of their discovery; and I have no doubt but that he has been hasty in his conclusions. At any rate, they are his individual

> opinions; and the Smithsonian does not propose to publish or endorse
> them in any way whatever. You can use them for what they are
> worth to you; possibly some assertions therein may show up some
> weak points in the arguments, and if they can be used to meet them,
> the better. (Baird 1877MS).

With a friend at court supporting the tablets, the Academy felt confirmed in their view of the authenticity. The next year Harrison and
Gass found the limestone tablet, and soon thereafter the elephant
pipes appeared; it would not be until 1883 that serious doubts about
the elephants would be raised by Henshaw of the Smithsonian Bureau
of Ethnology. In 1885-86, Cyrus Thomas of the same institution published a critical evaluation of the tablets, but these appraisals were
delayed by temporizing. Had a corrected and somewhat modified report been issued by Foreman, some of the charges later raised in discussion would have been clarified from the beginning.

The Mormon Theory

It was so difficult to accept the inscribed tablets that other explanations were used by some to avoid questioning the discoveries by Gass.
One of these alternatives, first discussed by Farquharson (1877a:65-
66), was the possibility of Mormons planting the tablets. Peet implied
the same solution to the dilemma in footnotes (1892:72; 1903:44).
Such a solution, clearing local members from guilt, still allowed the
tablets to be rejected as spurious. We may suspect the influence of
Foreman's manuscript upon Farquharson. Unfortunately, he soon left
for a position in Des Moines where he died in 1884, and his cautions
were no longer of weight within the Academy. The way was now open
for extreme, far ranging views.

Hittites, Noah's Ark, and Dakota Indians

4

In the early 1880s, other scholars, accepting the authenticity of the tablets, grappled with the problems of interpreting the inscriptions. One of these scholars published an analysis announcing that the symbols were syllabic and allied to Japanese, Chinese, and Korean. According to him, the designs represented a "sacrificial festivity" and a record of the "Noachian deluge" (Seyffarth 1882:75, 77). Another man compared the Davenport inscriptions with Hittite hieroglyphics that "furnished us with the key to reading of this inscription of the moundbuilders. . . ." (Campbell 1882:145). A third approach was supplied by Horatio N. Rust who consulted the Dakota Indians. They informed him that the so-called writing had no meaning and was merely ornamental.

The rival decipherments typify an era when the most unfounded and speculative nonsense was regularly published in the leading scientific journals. Whatever the archaeological validity of the finds might prove to be, the discussions interpreting them became incredible, as the three following examples illustrate.

Noah and the Ark

Professor Seyffarth of Philadelphia received a copy of volume 2 of the Davenport *Proceedings* containing the account of the tablets by Farquharson and others. Immediately recognizing their great importance, he wrote in an article published in volume 3 of the *Proceedings* of the Davenport Academy that these were ". . . the first discovered phonetic and astronomic monuments of the primitive inhabitants of this country, which, sooner or later, will cast unexpected light upon the origin, the history, the religion, the language, the science and intellectual faculties of our ancient Indians." (Seyffarth 1882:72). He, himself, could not decipher the inscription but noted that the "harmony of the Iowa, Mexican and South American [*sic*] characters puts beyond question that all the primitive inhabitants of America must have descended from the same aborigines. . . . It is self-evident that America must have been populated by the next nations, of course by the Japanese, Coreans, and Chinese. This conclusion is justified by the 15 Indian letters, corresponding with Chinese, Corean, and Japanese ones. . . ." (Ibid., 73). These interpretations permitted Professor Seyffarth to conclude that:

> We return to the reliable results obtained by the unparalleled Davenport antiquities, of which the following are the most important ones:
>
> 1. The primitive inhabitants of North America were no preadamites, nor offsprings of the monkeys, but Noachites.
> 2. They belonged to the same nation by which Mexico and South America were populated after the dispersion of the nations in 2780 B.C.
> 3. The literature of the American Indians evidences that they emigrated from Japan, or Corea, or proper China.
> 4. They must have come over prior to the year 1597 B.C.
> 5. Our Indians, as well as those in Mexico and South America, knew the history of the deluge, especially that Noah's family then consisted of eight persons.
> 6. The primitive inhabitants of America were much more civilized than our present Indian tribes.
> 7. The former understood the art of writing, and used a great many of syllabic characters, based upon the Noachian alphabet, and from the left to the right hands, like the Chinese.
> 8. They were acquainted with the seven planets and the twelve signs of the Zodiac, and they referred the same stars to the same constellations as did the Chaldeans, Egyptians, Greeks, Romans, etc.
> 9. They had solar years and solar months, even twelve hours of the day. They knew the cardinal points of the Zodiac, and the cardinal days of the year.
> 10. Their religion agreed with that of the Babylonians, Egyptians, Assyrians, Greeks, Romans, etc., because they worshipped the planets and the twelve gods of the Zodiac by sacrifices. Compare Isaiah [Jeremiah] 51, 7: "Babylon hath been a golden cup in the Lord's hand that made all the earth drunken; the nations have been drunken of her wine; therefore the nations are mad." (Ibid., 80).

As a final word about the preceding interpretations, one should refer to Robert Wauchope's excellent book *Lost Tribes and Sunken Continents: Myth and Method in the Study of American Indians* (1962). Far ranging Israelite or equivalent migrations were repeatedly introduced as mystic explanations for the presence of the indigenous populations. Seyffarth had excavated in Europe as a young man, first publishing in 1825, becoming more speculative in his subsequent articles. He was a very old man in 1881 when he advanced the Noah and Great Deluge explanation of the tablets. From this perspective, he represented the culmination, but not the end, of mythical analogy in archaeological interpretation.

Hittites and Human Sacrifice

Among the various theories of the tablets, only one scholar succeeded in actually proposing a decipherment of the difficult inscription itself. John Campbell of Montreal published an article in the *American Antiquarian* in 1882. His account opens with the statement that Hittite hieroglyphics furnish a key to this inscription of the mound builders. There is, of course, an immediate problem since Hittite was itself undeciphered, and for this reason Campbell reviews his own solution to this particular difficulty before continuing to the Davenport tablets. After briefly reviewing his previously published assertions about the Hittite origins of many of the American tribes, Campbell states that he was able to determine the phonetic value of 25 characters "chiefly through the Aztec, but also, to a certain extent by means of the Cypriote [Eastern Mediterranean], which Professor Sayce regards as the cursive descendant of the Hittite hieroglyphic system." (Campbell 1882:145). The Cremation Scene tablet can thus be deciphered, and after some verbal gymnastics it is read and then interpreted:

> We may regard Sataba as justly incurring the penalty of death for murder, but it is hard to say why the maiden Sapoca and Alcaalisca, who was probably the son of Alpi, should have suffered at the same time. The expression, in the men, in the women, the maiden, boys *poma utica* would seem to convey the idea that the sacrifices were offered on their behalf, or in order that Caal, the god might be propitious to them. It is interesting in this connection to compare the first line of the fourth Hittite inscription from Hamath, . . . sacrificed the chief Caba to Baal. The Hittites of Syria seem, either to have neglected the worship of their national divinities or to have adored them under Semitic names. . . . It may be some time yet before our knowledge of the Hittite language will enable us to arrive at perfectly accurate translations of their inscriptions. Nor does it matter very much for the present that a few words in the Davenport tablet which cannot affect the sense of the reading to any great extent remain a mystery. Were its language altogether unknown, it would still, as a purely Hittite monument, link the Old World with the New, destroy many false ethnological theories, and prove a stepping stone to a truer science of the past in this continent. (Ibid., 151, 153).

How the Hittites Reached America

In a summary abstract published the next year in the *Transactions* of the American Association for the Advancement of Science, Campbell described a very hypothetical route by which the "Khita or Kheti" [Neo-Hittites?] reached America. His identifications partially rested upon his translation and identification of the Davenport tablets.

> The Khitan empire existed on the borders of Palestine and Syria in the fifteenth century B.C., and was destroyed by the Assyrian Sargon in the year 717 B.C. Soon afterwards it was reëstablished in northern India where Alexander found it still flourishing in 327 B.C. Aryan encroachments did not succeed in wholly overturning this empire till the fourth century A.D. Then it revived in Chorasmia and after a short existence removed its seat on account of Tartar invasions to Siberia. Another eastward movement, the result of foreign pressure, marked the eighth and ninth centuries, during which period Corea and Japan must have been colonized and America discovered. In the eighth century the Toltec empire in Mexico began, and in the eleventh the Aztecs left their Asiatic home . . . translations of several of these inscriptions, Hittite, Siberian and Mound-builder [were published by Campbell], the key to their transliteration being the Aztec hieroglyphic system and to their translation the Japanese language, which he regarded as the standard of Khitan speech . . . the Sanscrit of American speech, by which the languages of apparently diverse origin might be unified as to source, must be looked for not in America, but in the old world. (Campbell 1883:420-421).

We may conclude Campbell's line of inquiry with the brief note that Hittite cuneiform inscriptions in Turkey were not to be successfully deciphered for thirty more years. It is a complicated matter because several languages are represented, but the main core of the inscriptions demonstrated conclusively that Hittite was an Indo-European language (see Gurney 1952: 117-131). Thus Campbell's earlier suggestion that the Japanese language was a "standard" or intermediate between the Eastern Mediterranean and the Mississippi Valley represents one of the ill-founded and preposterous confusions characteristic of some of the scholarship a century ago.

Dakota Indian Interpretation

In 1882, Horatio N. Rust of Pasadena, California, published an abstract of his views in the *Proceedings of the American Association for the Advancement of Science*. Given in its entirety:

> Believing that the pictures on the Davenport Tablets lack evidence of great antiquity, and are the work of the Indians who were re-

cent Moundbuilders, I took representations of the Tablets to the Dakotas, showing them to several of the older members of the tribe, telling them how they were found, and asking what they meant. The answers were in each instance substantially the same and without hesitation, viz.:

That the picture of the "mound" represents an earth lodge, in which a dance was being held.

The "prostrate forms" represented those persons who were overcome by the efforts and excitement of the dance.

The "curling smoke" arose from a fire in the lodge, indicating that the dance was held in cold weather.

The "moon and stars" signify that the dance was conducted in the night.

The "upright marks" around the lodge represent a fence of sticks set in the ground. A common custom among them today.

The irregular markings which some persons have tried to interpret as evidence of a written language, were simply ornamental markings conveying no intelligence.

Similar earth lodges destroyed by time and other causes have formed many mounds and groups of mounds, which now may be seen upon the benches all along the Missouri River. (Rust 1882:584-585).

The view of the Indians that burial mounds were ancient earth lodges resolved the mound-builder problem in an unusual way, as did the elimination of the writing as a meaningful inscription. Yet Rust stood virtually alone in denying that writing was present. Most observers interpreted the markings as symbolic characters among which Roman numerals could be discerned.

The Storm Breaks

5

The professional journals viewed the discoveries with caution. In the *American Naturalist,* Otis T. Mason went so far as to warn the Academy against the dangers of being "duped by some wag." (1878:322). There were various rejoinders and comments in that journal and others. The director of the U.S. Bureau of Ethnology, Major John W. Powell, was deeply concerned about the growing number of frauds and the unfounded speculations they created. He specifically cautioned against "enthusiastic theorists" and "blind zeal" which rejected the simple hypothesis of a continuous prehistoric Indian population. (Powell 1883). This warning appeared in the introduction to the *Second Annual Report* of the bureau and one of the following papers, "Animal Carvings from Mounds of the Mississippi Valley," specifically attacked the Academy specimens. Written by Henry Henshaw, the discussion opened a raging controversy, and instead of casting doubt on the specimens, indirectly made them famous.

Henshaw's Attack on the Elephants

Henshaw's study examined the problem of identifying the animals represented on the carved pipes. If the animals were not local species, it would add weight to theories that the mound builders came from some other region. If local species were exclusively represented, it would support the opinion that mound builders were long native to the area. Since there were reports identifying so-called foreign, non-indigenous animals on effigy pipes, the whole problem required review.

By training, Henshaw was an ornithologist and consequently was singularly well equipped for the identifications. His major conclusion was that the animals represented indigenous local species. It provided no support for lost race theories.

The two unique elephant pipes represented a special problem, for it was unclear when the mastodon became extinct. There was, he added, no proof that the mound builders were contemporaneous with mastodon. This led him to a discussion of the elephant pipes, tablets, and the Reverend Jacob Gass. Although his discussion raised a legitimate issue, his tone was supercilious and belittling. That one man should

find both unique pipes raised "suspicion," particularly when great activity by other mound explorers in the same region had found nothing
like them. The "remarkable archaeologic instinct" and his "divining
rod" led the same man to find "remarkable" tablets. Henshaw then al-
luded to archaeological fraud:

> Bearing in mind the many attempts at archaeological frauds that
> recent years have brought to light, archaeologists have a right to
> demand that objects which afford a basis for such important de-
> ductions as the coeval life of the Mound-Builder and the mastodon,
> should be above the slightest suspicion not only in respect to their
> resemblances, but as regards the circumstances of discovery. If
> they are not above suspicion, the science of archaeology can better
> afford to wait for further and more certain evidence than to commit
> itself to theories which may prove stumbling-blocks to truth until
> that indefinite time when future investigations shall show their il-
> lusory nature. (Henshaw 1883:158).

In reading this article today, one is impressed by a basically reasonable
position. It was a remarkable coincidence that one man should find so
much and such unique artifacts while others found nothing. It did
make good sense to defer elaborate theories until substantiating finds
could be obtained from other excavations. Unfortunately, Henshaw
had included some unpleasant words. His repeated allusion to suspicions was not reinforced with any evidence. It could be regarded as a
personal attack upon the integrity of Gass even though he was not
mentioned by name. To those who read his paper, Henshaw appeared as a partisan and it damaged his case.

Putnam to the Rescue

When Henshaw's "insinuations and slanders" reached the Academy
there was considerable commotion and a special meeting. A leading
member took the job of writing a reply. It was published and widely
circulated in 1885, with a longer version appearing the next year.
The author, Charles E. Putnam, who served two terms as president of
the Academy, was an extremely wealthy local businessman and collector. His gifts to the Academy included important collections of art
and scientific specimens from many parts of the world. His talented
son who died young had been one of the mainsprings of investigation
in the natural sciences, and Putnam's wife was very prominent in
Academy affairs. The Putnam family later richly endowed the Academy and its successor, the Davenport Public Museum. To Putnam, the

statements by Henshaw were outrageous, unthinkable, and debased the scientific work of the Academy. Putnam suspected a plot stemming from the Smithsonian Institution to destroy the Academy itself. He believed that Powell was determined to prove that the mound builders were just Indians, rather than a lost race, by deliberately destroying the credibility of all the valid evidence that did not support his theory. Henshaw, Powell's employee, was carrying out his attacks on the unique Academy specimens as part of this scheme.

Putnam's defense (1886) appears in detail in a 95-page appendix to the *Proceedings,* beginning with the bitter note that it is a "vindication of the authenticity of the elephant pipes and inscribed tablets in the museum of the Davenport Academy . . . from the accusations of the Bureau of Ethnology of the Smithsonian Institution." It is an interesting document. Taken by itself without reference to other facts, it is surprisingly convincing and well written. Putnam's argument runs along the following lines: Henshaw is an ornithologist, not an archaeologist, and he did not study the specimens or visit the sites. Henshaw did not talk to those who witnessed the discoveries—men of good character and social position who would not participate in frauds. In his publication, Henshaw used a highly inaccurate drawing reproduced in an eastern magazine and erred when describing the circumstances of recovery and the specimens themselves; for example, stating that the elephants lacked tails when in fact tails were present on the elephant pipes. Besides, how could anyone insert a fraud into a completely frozen mound with witnesses present? Thus, Putnam wrote that Henshaw maligned the excellent character of Jacob Gass and his associates and calumniated the scientific work of the Academy by his base, unfounded, and completely unsubstantiated charges.

Damning the Smithsonian

When the defense "Elephant Pipes and Inscribed Tablets . . ." was published and widely circulated in 1885, letters inundated the Davenport Academy. Most of the correspondence was highly favorable to the Academy position. Charles E. Putnam, with the permission of the writers, published a large number of these comments as a thirty-page addendum to the report when it was reissued the next year. He published, we might add, both the favorable and the few noncommittal responses "in order that both sides may be fairly presented." (Putnam 1886:300). The following selections illuminate the emotions aroused by the question of mound builder origins. Dr. Edwin Hamilton Davis of New York, coauthor of the famous report by Squier and Davis published in 1848 as the first volume of *Smithsonian Contributions to Knowledge,* wrote Putnam:

> I consider it a triumphant refutation of the accusations of Mr. Henshaw and the absurd theories of the Bureau of Ethnology in the Smithsonian Institution. (Ibid., 300).

The other letters published by Putnam also denounced or decried the Smithsonian. Some excerpts by various men illustrate the level of discussion (Putnam 1886:300-317):

> Dr. D. B. Brinton, Philadelphia, Penn.:
> I considered it a paper not composed in the true spirit of science and out of place in the publications of the Bureau.

> Prof. Alexander Winchell, Ann Arbor, Mich.:
> I fear there has been some hasty dogmatizing in Washington.

> S. A. Miller, Cincinnati, Ohio:
> They had no warrant for their attack and you were justified throughout in exposing them.

> Rev. J. P. MacLean, Hamilton, Ohio:
> You certainly have literally annihilated Henshaw, and it is to be hoped that he will at once retire into the obscurity from which Major Powell has dragged him forth, and that his like may never again be seen in the land.

> A. C. Webber, Decatur, Illinois:
> Your ably-written paper has the effect of a thunderbolt upon the stagnant insinuations of Mr. Henshaw. It purifies the cause of ethnology.

> Charles H. Stubbs, M.D., Wakefield, Penn.:
> Jejune writers are prone to be hypercritical, and he seems to be no exception to the general rule.

> A. E. Blair, Castle Creek, N.Y.:
> His attack upon the Academy was, to say the least, unprovoked and ungentlemanly.

> W. A. Chapman, Okolona, Arkansas:
> The defense of Mr. Gass is the defense of all private investigators.

> S. A. Brinkley, Alexandria, Ohio:
> Nor is Major Powell exempt from censure in permitting this mass of cruel insinuations to go forth.

> A. Dean, High Bridge, N.J.:
> I find it impossible to account for the seeming complicity of the Smithsonian in the assault.

Edward L. Berthoud, Golden, Colo.:
> I know something of Mr. Henshaw and I think he has "brass" enough in him in thus settling, *ex cathedra*, what has puzzled and foiled the repeated attempts of some of the best antiquarians.

Max Uhle, Dresden, Prussia:
> . . . and it is to be wondered at that so eager attacks are undertaken as to the authenticity of relics without any inspection of the things themselves.

Dr. Willis De Hass, Washington, D.C.:
> The elephant pipes, which have elicited so much criticism, I consider as genuine as the most undoubted specimens in the museum. Subjected to the sharpest tests, they pass successfully.

The masterly lawyer's defense by Putnam blunted the issue of the genuineness of the specimens by publicly proclaiming the integrity of Gass and the other members of the Academy, and then questioning the motives of Henshaw. With this approach, he had obtained great sympathy from miscellaneous gentlemen across the country who were interested in archaeology, from many scholars, and from various journals of the period.

Reaction in the Journals

In the second edition of his defense, Putnam included a selection of initially favorable reviews entitled "Criticisms of Scientific Journals." In the *American Antiquarian,* the editor, Stephen Peet, had written: "The more we read Mr. Henshaw's article, the more pretentious and groundless do the positions of the writer seem. There is scarcely a truthful or convincing paragraph in the whole article. . . . The article is destined to produce mischief and arouse prejudice against the Bureau. Mr. Henshaw evidently owes an apology to the Davenport Society." (Putnam 1886:334-335).

Dr. Stephen Bowers, in the May issue of the *Pacific Science Monthly,* expressed his opinions colloquially, writing that "Mr. Putnam replies in an incisive way that will doubtless cause the Washington relic sharps to look a "leedle out". . . . The *savants* of Washington have doubtless been hasty in their condemnation of the finds we have been considering." (Ibid., 335).

The July 1885 issue of the *American Naturalist* supports Putnam's defense. "The article is racy reading, and incidentally gives strong arguments against the desire for centralization in science shown in certain quarters. It will be found impossible to concentrate all science in any

one clique or city. Our local societies and scattered observers need
not feel that their efforts are not as valuable in their way as the labors
of Government officials and closet or office naturalists." (Ibid., 338).
The *American Journal of Science* in May 1885 presented its readers
with a lengthy summary of Putnam's defense, quoting him directly.
There was no editorial comment, and his conclusions stood without
rebuttal. (Ibid., 339-341).

The prestigious English periodical *Nature* took up the question in the
issue of 16 April 1885. After discussing the scientific questions involved, it concludes, "The whole subject is one of extraordinary interest, and Mr. Putnam's statement, vouched as it is by a formal resolution of the Davenport Academy, must play an important part in any
subsequent discussion as to the value to be attached to these remains,
which, if authentic, are acknowledged to have much influence on the
final settlement of the question as to who the Mound-builders were."
(Ibid., 341).

Circumstances of Discovery

6

To those unaware of the intricacies of the problem, Putnam's defense, together with his compilation of letters and journal reviews, restored the authenticity of the specimens. The longer 1886 version, however, appeared at a difficult time. Even before it circulated, several new crises faced the Academy.

The entanglements of the controversy are presented sequentially, although they appeared more or less together in various journals spaced over a period of six months in the winter and following spring of 1886. One line of attack concerned the validity of the inscribed tablets and the circumstances of discovery. The arguments pro and con that appeared in *Science* form the subject of this chapter; chapter 7 presents a second line of attack, in the *American Antiquarian,* concerning the strange transactions of the Reverend Jacob Gass; chapters 8 and 9 consider a third line of debate, eventually appearing in the *Proceedings* and manuscripts of the Academy and centering upon the division of membership over the authenticity of the specimens.

Cyrus Thomas Cites a Letter

Professor Cyrus Thomas, a colleague of Henshaw and the director of archaeological explorations for the Bureau of Ethnology, had suspicions of fraud since the year 1882. In December 1885, Putnam having forced his hand, Thomas published a note in *Science* concerning the limestone tablet (plate 4). Not only was the tablet itself anomalous, being "discovered" in 1878, with an engraved figure eight in both Arabic and Roman numerals, but the stratigraphy had evidence of recent disturbance. The original excavation report noted that the removal of a rough limestone slab revealed a cavity beneath it, and the "engraved tablet *was suddenly exposed to view.*" (plate 16). In order to be certain, Thomas had written to the curator, Pratt, who replied, "Mr. C. E. Harrison, who assisted in the work, states that the cavity in which the limestone tablet was found *contained scarcely any dirt.*" Thomas continued:

> that there should have been an unfilled space in a pile of loose stone
> in an excavation, beneath a heap of comparatively loose dirt which

had stood there for centuries, is certainly most extraordinary.

In a letter now in my possession, written by Mr. A. S. Tiffany in 1882, I find the following statement: "The limestone tablet I am certain is a fraud. Mr. Gass was assisted in digging it out by Mr. Harrison and Mr. Hume. Mr. Hume informs me that there was a wall of small bowlders around the tablet. On the tablet there were some arrow-points, a quartz crystal, and a Unio shell filled with red paint, the whole being covered with a rough limestone slab, *the space between it and the tablet not filled with earth, and the paint bright and clean.*" Mr. Tiffany was one of the founders of the Academy, and, as appears from the Proceedings, was long one of its most prominent, active, and trusted local members, and is still a member. . . .

It is proper to add here that Mr. Tiffany, in the same letter, vouches for the honesty of Mr. Gass (the finder), who, he believes, was deceived. Speaking of the elephant pipe found by Mr. Gass, which he also thinks was a plant, he says, "It bears the same finger-marks as the first one [first pipe], and Mr. Gass could be deceived with that plant as he was with the tablet. Mr. Gass is honest." I have Mr. Tiffany's acknowledgment that this letter, which has been in my possession since 1882, is authentic. (Thomas 1885:564).

A Reconsideration of the Slate Tablets

Rejecting the limestone tablet and elephant pipes, Cyrus Thomas continued the attack. In the next issue of *Science,* 1 January 1886, Thomas described features of the Hunting Scene, Cremation Scene and Calendar tablets "calculated to arouse suspicion."

The Cremation Scene tablet had among the various characters three examples of Arabic numeral eights, like those on the limestone tablet. An animal-like concretion with inset quartz crystal eyes (plate 16) was afterwards found in backdirt from the excavation of Mound 3 where the slate tablets were found. The limestone tablet from Mound 11 had quartz inset eyes in the representations of effigy pipes. (See plate 4). Thomas concluded that the figure eights, other symbolism, and quartz inset eyes linked together the tablets from the excavations of 1877 and 1878. "It is thus almost impossible to avoid the conclusion that all must stand or fall together." (Thomas 1886:10).

Relative to the archaeological context of the Mound 3 finds, Thomas notes the disturbed nature of the skeletons, a point first raised by Foreman (1877MSa). Grave *A*, excavated in 1874, had undisturbed burials, in contrast with the disorder Gass encountered in grave *B*, when the tablets were found in 1877. (See plate 15).

Finally, Thomas suggested a source for the hieroglyphic inscriptions. Webster's unabridged dictionary, 1872 edition, page 1766, illustrated the letters of the various Old World alphabets. The resemblance of letters from this page to examples found on the inscriptions "in most cases is very strong. The reader can make the comparison for himself." As for the Calendar stone (plate 3) Webster's dictionary on page 1704 illustrated a zodiac very similar to it with four concentric zones and twelve signs. "The question of the authenticity of these relics should, if possible, be definitely settled, as they have, if genuine, an important bearing on some troublesome archaeological problems." (Thomas 1886:10-11).

Putnam's Rejoinder

Within two weeks of reading the exposé by Cyrus Thomas, Putnam had prepared his lawyer's brief in support and sent it off to *Science,* where it appeared 5 February 1886. We need do little more with it than summarize the main line of argument. Putnam's opening paragraph describes Thomas in these terms: "Probably no writer ever before set out to prepare a piece of 'destructive criticism' with so frank a confession of his disqualification for the task." Relative to the curious resemblance between the inscription and signs found in Webster's dictionary, Putnam indignantly replied, "These are fair specimens of the arguments by which Professor Thomas attempts to controvert the unimpeached statements of the discoverers. The resemblances indicated are so trivial and purely fanciful as to scarcely attain the level of serious criticism." Relative to the suspicion of recent placement of the limestone tablet in an empty chamber free of dirt, Putnam said, "Apparently no good reason can be given why a vault so protected from above, as well as at the sides, could not remain empty for ages."

Relative to another matter, "Professor Thomas makes this secret letter of Mr. Tiffany's the cornerstone of his argument. . . . I speak advisedly when I state that the quotation used by him is not correctly given. There are in it no less than four alterations of the text. . . . Nor is this all. . . . I am therefore compelled to pronounce the use made of this letter by Professor Thomas as unfair, and his quotations from it as garbled. I would not willingly do him any injustice, and hence now call upon him to publish this letter *verbatim et literatim.* . . . I am prepared to say that such publication would not only destroy its value as authority, but would subject Professor Thomas himself to censure in resorting to such sources for scientific material. . . . Apparently our Washington friends are so anxious to condemn, they are afraid to investigate." (Putnam 1886a:119-120).

No Need for Further Investigation

Putnam's charges against Cyrus Thomas and Tiffany were published in *Science* on 5 February. Thomas became so incensed that he immediately wrote a reply published the same month in *Science*, 26 February 1886. It begins, "Please allow me to trouble you once more, and finally, in reference to the Davenport tablets." (Thomas 1886a:189).

His first objection dealt with the Putnam reference to the Grave Creek tablet to establish the authenticity of the Davenport tablets. Thomas mentioned that contemporary archaeologists had generally rejected the Grave Creek specimen as spurious. Thomas then defended Tiffany against aspersions of illiteracy and detailed the various Academy offices and duties which he had filled. "Mr. Tiffany expresses entire confidence in the shale tablets, which is proof that his expression of doubt in regard to the 'limestone tablet' was not for the purpose of 'defaming his old associates,' but because the evidence satisfied him it was a plant." (Ibid.).

The lack of dirt in the stone vault where the limestone tablet was found is again mentioned. It would have been "a miracle if water had failed to enter the vault, and, in the course of centuries, fill it with dirt." (Ibid.). Thomas then reviewed the literature showing that he is "not alone in expressing doubts as to the authenticity of these tablets." In conclusion, he had not accepted the invitation to visit Davenport because, "If this evidence leads to the conclusion that these relics are modern productions, as I believe it does, there is no necessity for the present of 'further investigation.'" (Ibid., 189-190). The affair, however, was far from closed.

The Trials of Jacob Gass

7

At the time of the Thomas-Putnam exchange in *Science,* some scholars reversed their previously favorable position and became convinced of the fraud. Among the most prominent of this group was the Reverend Stephen Peet, who in his position as editor of the *American Antiquarian* published some highly damning testimony about the affairs of the Reverend Jacob Gass and other suspicious circumstances surrounding the discoveries. The published attacks had begun to shift from the unfortunate Henshaw to the explorer Gass.

The Doubts of Peet

In the January 1886 issue of the *American Antiquarian,* two weeks after the Academy's investigation committee was formed to inquire into Tiffany's behavior, Stephen Peet dropped a bombshell. He published an editorial entitled "Are the Davenport Tablets Frauds?", an eleven-page discussion with illustrations of anomalies in the inscriptions and with diagrams from the original excavation reports. Peet argued that the tablets appeared in a disturbed archaeological context and should be considered intrusive.

The excavation reports themselves provided "evidence that deception has been practiced and that 'a plant' has been perpetrated." He concluded his editorial with an intriguing statement about the number of inscribed tablets found by Gass. In addition to the Cook Farm limestone and slate tablets, through a remarkable coincidence Gass had found *five* others. These inscribed stones reported in the *Proceedings* (Gass 1877c:142) came from a creek bed some twenty-two miles west of Davenport. Peet disclaimed any

> intent to reflect upon the discoverer, for we have heretofore been, and are now, ready to defend him from all aspersions as to personal character and reputation, but the statement of facts in the very language of the Report is given with the question whether some unknown person has not been engaged in the work of planting tablets in the vicinity of Davenport, and whether various parties have not been misled? The tablets are too numerous and the discoveries too frequent for the majority of scientific men to accept them as genuine. (Peet 1886:56).

The inscribed stones from the creek bed were never illustrated. The largest was left in place but several were brought back by Gass and given to the museum. A search of the Davenport Museum collections in 1969 can find no trace of them.

The Curator Enters the Fray

The curator of the Davenport Academy and a highly regarded member of that organization, W. H. Pratt, angrily replied in the next month's issue of the *American Antiquarian*. The article "The Davenport Tablets Genuine" condemns Peet for "seeking to create suspicions," misunderstanding, and misinterpreting the "commonplace" circumstances of discovery. Pratt, after covering old ground, continued:

> It evidently makes no sort of difference any way, what is or what is not on the tablets, all circumstances are alike suggestive of the one idea which possesses our critics; the wish is father to the thought. If they would lay aside their fraud-glasses and use their natural faculties while not too much impaired, might they not see less "darkly". . . .
>
> Upon the appearance of these aggressive, systematic and persistent attacks upon the Davenport discoveries, the thought which naturally arises in the minds of readers every where, is the very pertinent question—which must some day be answered—*Whence* this desperate and blind eagerness to impeach the genuineness of these particular specimens? What are the considerations which prompt such reckless and ill-considered efforts, upon the most frivolous pretexts, and by perversion of facts, feeble puerilities and obviously false inferences, to arouse suspicion and to manufacture public opinion? (Pratt 1886:94).

The reply to the curator appeared in the March issue of the *American Antiquarian*. Peet, in his editorial entitled "The Points Involved," reiterated his previous conclusions and dismissed the curator's objections by saying, ". . . the method of argument which the writer uses is not one which we admire." (Peet 1886a:118). He then published some incredible letters and a rejoinder by an amateur, A. F. Berlin, which conclusively demonstrated that Gass had traded fraudulent relics to a private collector.

Gass Linked With Other Frauds

The finger of suspicion again pointed at Gass. The enthusiastic collector was the only man present at all of the tablet excavations, and he helped obtain the first elephant pipe specimen from its owner, a local farmer. In defense of the clergyman, Putnam wrote:

> . . . the principal discoverer of the inscribed tablets belonged to this select circle of voluntary workers, and that, in his own home, his word was beyond question and his character above reproach. In this connection it may properly be stated that Mr. Gass, who, as the discoverer of these unique relics, is assailed by Mr. Henshaw, is now preaching to a congregation at Postville, in Northern Iowa, where he is, as he everywhere has been, highly esteemed by his people. He is a good classical scholar, well grounded in Hebrew, but with a decided scientific bent of mind, which accounts for his perseverance and enthusiasm in these archaeological explorations. It would seem that his fine abilities, extensive attainments, high social position, and spotless character should have shielded him from attack; and if, peradventure, it ever falls to the lot of his assailants to themselves encounter "destructive criticism", it will then serve them in good stead should they be able to confront it with as clean a record. (Putnam 1886:274).

When Putnam's defense of the clergyman appeared, including the statement about his character, a collector in Pennsylvania, A. F. Berlin, immediately wrote off a heated reply to the *American Antiquarian* which Peet published with the editorial. Was Gass a learned man of letters? Berlin, who published some correspondence by Gass, "corrected the spelling." Berlin's purpose is to discuss the transaction in which Gass sent clearly fraudulent specimens to H. C. Stevens of Oregon in 1881, before Henshaw's attack. Berlin is convincing. He had possession of the Gass correspondence and the frauds themselves. Gass seems to have been a local trader in antiquities of a most dubious nature. Berlin discussed some of the specimens which Gass traded out of state:

> I take the liberty to describe the articles, though they need only to be seen to be known as fraudulent. The first is a pipe-shaped object . . . *and is made from white marble,* originally covered with lead-colored paint. This has worn off, and shows the nature of the stone. The fraud was exposed still more by the application of spirits of turpentine. . . . The next pipe is a close grained stone which completed is to represent the head and neck of a bird. . . . The marks made by a file can be plainly seen on this object. . . . The third pipe, also of a fine grained stone, is to represent a primitive form of mound pipe. . . . File marks are also perceptible here. . . . In the lot are two flat, oblong pieces of red shale . . . [each one marked on the label] as "aboriginal money from Illinois". . . . The last in this collection is a flat, oblong object called a "Sacrificial Plate," having a spoon-shaped groove almost covering

one side. There is along one end on the other side a well defined, curved projection forming at an angle with the depression which I suppose was meant for a handle. (Berlin 1886:99-100).

The Gass-Stevens Correspondence

In addition to describing the specimens, Berlin (1886:101) published the correspondence. The letter below was written by Mr. Gass and is followed by Mr. Stevens' reply:

Postville, Ia., Jan. 30, 1886

Mr. Stevens, Oregon City
Dear Sir:
I learned by letters of Mr. Berlin, at Allentown, Pa., sent to the Academy of Natural Science at Davenport that the Indian pipe I exchanged with you some years ago is not authentical and very doubtful just as you wrote to me when you received it. I am very sorry I did not believe you and that I was so badly mistaken. I got the whole lot sent to you from the same party and now I am afraid there could be some more doubtful articles among them and of course I never would give to any body a doubtful relic by my will and knowledge. In this case I think it would be my honor and duty to correct my mistake and send you your specimens back again by mail today and you also will be so kindly and send mine back to me. Enclosed I send you hereby postal note 50 cents, by postage, to send my lot back by mail. Should the postage be higher I will send you the balance.

Resp. Yours,

J. Gass

Oregon City, Oregon, Feby. 9, '86.

Rev. J. Gass
Dear Sir:
Your letter dated Jan'y 30th, and enclosing postal note for 50 cents to hand. The box you mention as having shipped is not yet to hand. When it does come both it and the order shall be held subject to your instructions, as the articles I received from you are not now in my possession. They now belong to Mr. Berlin of Allentown, Pa. I am sorry to say that not only the pipe, but the pipes, and each and every other article received from you, were the basest kind of frauds. Now, it seems to me that a man of your reputation would hardly be so easily imposed upon by such worthless trash. If you have really been imposed upon, I am sorry, but it is now, I think, too late for me to do anything.

Yours truly,

H. C. Stevens   (Berlin 1886:101)

The remarks by Gass, including the statement "not authentical [*sic*] and very doubtful" seem impossibly weak when confronted by Stevens' reply ". . . each and every other article received from you, were the basest kind of frauds." We wonder, as Stevens did, how Gass could be so easily fooled.

The artifacts which Gass traded to Stevens are no longer in existence, to the best of my knowledge. However, the character of the specimens is rather well described by Berlin, as previously quoted. We may be reasonably certain of their spurious nature. This view is supported by other evidence. Berlin shrewdly sent the specimens to the Smithsonian to be identified so that it would not be his unsupported word as to their nature. In the Berlin correspondence (1886MS) there is a transcribed copy of the letter that Cyrus Thomas wrote to Berlin on 21 December 1885 about the specimens. Thomas wrote:

> I will take good care of the specimens, have them drawn for you and send you the drawings and specimens as soon as they are ready. I have no doubt that all but one, the one you name "a sacrificial stone" are frauds, unless possibly the red shale ornaments, which may be something made by the Indians or other persons merely for amusement. I have always been inclined to think Mr. Gass straight, but there can be no excuse for a man who has had any experience with mound relics putting off such specimens as these as genuine.
>
> I think I can show clearly that the limestone tablet found by him is a fraud, but I think he was cheated in it. (Thomas in Berlin 1886MS).

The Gass Defense

Before the storm of criticism, Gass had taken a new position at Postville in northeast Iowa, resigning as a trustee of the Academy in January 1883. Possibly his Davenport parishioners had objected to his spending so much time at the mound excursions. At the time of recriminations, he was working at various mounds in Allamakee and other counties and is mentioned from time to time in the *Proceedings* as donating a few specimens or sending a note on his activities. The news of the existence of the Gass-Stevens correspondence had been intimated by Peet as early as November 1885. When it was published in March of the next year, Putnam was furious. In an unpublished letter dated 20 April Putnam (1886MS) wrote Peet that the defense of Gass rested upon his inability to express himself in English. The letters sent out under the signature of Gass had been dictated by him to his students and not thoroughly read before being mailed. Peet replied that he would only publish the Gass defense if it were sent to him directly by Gass himself. If it was in German, Peet would have it translated.

His reluctance, it appears, stemmed from having a defense manufactured by Putnam at the Academy. "Mr. Gass has the right to be heard, but he will be heard in his own name and not through a lawyer who is seeking to catch me and make me trouble." (Peet 1886MS).

There is documentary substantiation that Putnam was seeking to intimidate Peet with threats of libel and secondly that a certain amount of collusion was present among Putnam, Pratt, and Gass in the preparation of the Gass statement. The threats against Peet appear in Peet (1886MS) and Jones (1886MS). The collusion is seen in the letter from Gass (1886MS) to Pratt.

With the *American Antiquarian* closed to him, Putnam turned to *Science,* where there appeared in May 1886 a lengthy rejoinder to the charges made by Berlin. Putnam wrote the introduction with his lawyer's skill. The items traded by Gass are "alleged fraudulent mound-relics." It is "plainly intimated that these disclosures tended to place all that gentleman's discoveries under the ban of suspicion." However, the publication of these letters was made without communicating with the Davenport Academy or "affording Mr. Gass an opportunity for explanation." Mr. Gass had an imperfect knowledge of English.

> It is always to be deplored when personal considerations enter into scientific discussions, but in archaeological research, where the question of the authenticity so largely depends upon the integrity of the explorer, character becomes an important factor, and is a legitimate subject for inquiry. In cases like that under consideration, however, this moral test should be sternly applied alike to the accuser and the accused. (Putnam 1886b:438).

Scarcely Require Any Special Assurance

Putnam's introduction was followed by a lengthy communication written to him by Gass, and the translation was certified as correct by two prominent German-speaking citizens of Davenport. In this narrative, Gass relates that the curator, Mr. Pratt, authorized him to undertake the exchange and that he sent off a box of "primitive" implements originally received from Pastor Mutschman of Missouri. He originally gave no credit to Stevens' complaints

> but took it for an empty excuse made in order to give me little or nothing for them. If I had entertained the *least* doubt of their

genuineness, I would not, under any circumstances, have sent them; or at least, after Mr. Stevens had made these remarks, I should certainly at once have asked [for] them, and taken them back at any price.

As to who has written my letters for me, I cannot now say positively. Mrs. Gass says it was certainly done by one of my pupils, and I believe she is right. A letter in German, written by myself, would surely have sounded quite differently. These unfortunate letters have, however, been sent in my name, and with my name, and I must now abide the consequences, come what will. I can scarcely understand, even now (supposing that Mr. Berlin's copy of my letter is correct), how the incorrect statement that the academy had bought such pipes, and paid such high prices for them, could have occurred unobserved. The boy who wrote the letter for me must have misunderstood me, and from my ignorance of the English language I overlooked this error. It may be, that, not attaching much importance to this letter, I may have sent it without first examining or looking it over. . . .

In regard to the relics in question, it is impossible at present for me to determine whether those which Mr. Stevens *claims* to have received from me are actually *the* objects which I have sent him; for I have not seen them as yet, and for the present shall have no opportunity, as Mr. Berlin has informed you that he could not send them for my inspection without the consent of Mr. Stevens. On the contrary, Mr. Stevens says that they no longer belong to him but to Mr. Berlin. . . .

That the intention or the thought of having any thing to do with doubtful relics, or of deceiving any one with them, was far from my mind, will to you, scarcely require any special assurance from me. (Gass in Putnam 1886b:438-439).

The above defense by Gass was not altogether spontaneous. A letter from Gass, dated Postville 13 April 1886, admits as much. In this communication addressed to Curator Pratt, Gass (1) acknowledges receipt of his own defense letter from the Academy; (2) he says, "I have in general left everything as it was" and only made minor changes; (3) adds, "In case you find it desirable to make any changes you may do so with entire freedom;" and (4) since the defense letter was written in German, Gass says he will recopy it, apparently to hide alterations, "Should it be necessary to copy the letter again, I will be ready at any time, but before Easter it would not be possible." (Gass 1886MS).

There is nothing wrong with reviewing a manuscript before publication—quite the contrary. The problem, however, is deciding what is Putnam and Pratt's influence in this defense allegedly written by Gass himself.

Tiffany's Ordeal

8

Charles E. Putnam repeatedly elaborated the argument that no one in the Academy doubted either the good faith of the discoverers or the genuineness of the unique specimens. Tiffany's letter to the Bureau of Ethnology destroyed this argument. Putnam responded by organizing the expulsion of Tiffany from the Academy; he set up a committee to investigate Tiffany's conduct. The success of Putnam illustrates the scientific weakness of the Davenport organization.

The Tiffany Letter

The crucial role of the Tiffany letter to the controversy has been described in the exchange between Cyrus Thomas and Putnam published in *Science* in late 1885 and early 1886. The real letter itself never appeared except in short excerpts. Putnam (1886a:119) challenged Thomas to publish it *verbatim et literatim*, saying such an action would destroy Tiffany's value as an authority and subject Thomas himself to "censure" for relying on such sources of information. The letter (Tiffany 1882MS) survives in copy and shows discrepancies on both sides of the exchange. Note the misspellings and lack of punctuation.

> NW 5th St Da[venport, Ia., Oct.]27 1882
>
> Prof P W Norris
> Dear Sir
> Your favor of Oct 23th at hand I would have liked to shown you several groups of mounds and the shell beds near milan Ills and some very rair symbals in my collection and had your opinion and large experiance in regard to their use and to have told you my opinion of the Tablets and the Eliphant pipes
> Those shale tablets I have the utmost confidence that they are genuine I examined the situation when they ware first obtained
> The limestone tablet I am certain is a fraud
> Mr Gass assisted in diging it out by Mr Harison and Mr John Hume Mr Hume informs me that there was a wall of small bowlders around the tablet on the tablet there was some arrow points a quartz crystal and a unio shell filled with red paint the whole being covered with a rough lime stone slab the space betwene it and the tabled not filled with earth and the paint bright and clean
> It is only nessisary to say that Mr Harison is a stone cutter

> In regard to the eliphant pipes would say that the first pipe has
> no no history it is made of a coal measure sand rock which is very
> soft and friable it is saturated with grease which gives it the ap-
> pearance of hardness and age the one which Mr. Gass dug from a
> mound is of the same material also saturated with grease it has
> the same finger marks as the first one and Mr Gass could be de-
> ceived with that plant as he was with the tablet Mr Gass is honest
> but he is not sharp
> All the mound builders pipes found in this vicinity with this one
> exception are made of Catlinite and also the Naples' pipes found by
> Judge Henderson wich Prof Rhaw pronounced to be made of Ola-
> vine harder than tempered steel
> I am loosing confidence in scientific authority and believe little
> except what I can verify with my own sences
> I am not working with our Academy nor doo I ever expect to
> Very Truly yours.
> *A S, Tiffany* (1882MS)

The descriptions of Gass as honest but not sharp, and Harrison as a
stonecutter were bound to have an impact. At the time of Tiffany's
expulsion, Harrison was a pharmacist, but he seems to have been employed in the former occupation at an earlier time, according to unpublished testimony by Tiffany and Lindley which was not refuted.
Putnam felt that the illiterate aspects of the letter weighed against its
credibility. Thomas, on the other hand, relied on it as a knowledgeable
local source. At the time it was written, Tiffany was feuding with the
Academy but later participated in some of its affairs. Taken by itself,
it had no value; but when added to growing evidence, it was devastat-
ing.

The Investigating Committee

A special committee was appointed to investigate Tiffany's conduct as
an Academy member. The five members had read Tiffany's letter to
Norris and wished to learn if his two statements could be confirmed:
(1) that the two elephant pipes were saturated with grease to give the
appearance of antiquity, and (2) that the limestone tablet was a
"plant." They also wished to learn whether some of the other stories
in circulation, but not written down, could be substantiated. Accordingly, they sent identical notices to Tiffany, the curator, Pratt, and the
three excavators of the limestone tablet—Mr. Harrison, Mr. Hume, and
the Reverend Mr. Gas [*sic*] requesting written statements.

In contrast to his 1882 letter, Tiffany's written defense (1886MS) to the committee is a more literate statement prepared and polished by his lawyer. It is seven pages long, and typewritten, double spaced, on legal size paper. Copies were given to each member of the committee and circulated to other members. The first written charges against Tiffany were for "impeaching the genuineness of very important relics" and putting into circulation grave charges against the honor of his associate members without first presenting his charges to the Academy. Tiffany replied:

> I do not claim to have absolute proof that these relics are not what is claim[ed] for them by the persons who presented them. . . . As to the second matter charged, viz. that I have circulated grave charges against the honor and good faith of associate members, I have to say. The only foundation for such a charge was obtained from a private letter written by me to Prof. P. W. Norris some years since. . ,. .
>
> When a private correspondence must needs be ransacked in order to obtain evidence that a certain statement has been made it is bad enough. But when after obtaining such things in that manner, the letter itself is hawked about for the express purpose of informing persons of its contents, it comes with very poor grace to seek to charge the responsibility of "circulating" it upon the writer. (Tiffany 1886MS:4-6).

In correspondence, Cyrus Thomas (1885MS) clearly states he will not send a copy of the letter to Putnam. He will only send a copy back to Tiffany himself who then can give it to Putnam if he so wishes. Putnam demanded the letter from Tiffany, received it, and *then* circulated it to the committee and others as the primary basis of charges. Harrison's threat of a libel suit was based on a copy of this same letter, since his name did not appear in the original Thomas article. Tiffany's lawyer, who represented him at the hearing, advised against discussing the frauds in any detail *unless* the threat of a libel suit from Harrison was removed. Harrison refused. Consequently, in order to protect himself, Tiffany gave no more information to the committee. (See PDANS 5: 219-220). His defense was muffled.

The Curator Reports to the Committee

Pratt, a long-time member, former president and, by this time, the full-time curator, intimately knew the men, specimens, and affairs of the Academy. His report, handwritten and four and one-half pages long, carried weight. Although judicious in his discussion, he could find no evidence to support Tiffany's written statements in the letter to Norris about the specimens. From this paper, we also learn about the unwritten charges Tiffany was making to some fellow members. Pratt (1886MS) begins his statements with the comment, "I do not recall any charges of fraud in reference to the elephant pipes or limestone tablet being made to the Academy, nor any particular conversation with Mr. Tiffany concerning doubts about them." Yet further on he says:

> I recollect Mr. Gass telling me, while the pipe was broken, that Mr. Tiffany wished to buy the pieces and offered $5.00 for them—I think that was the amount, and very soon after he called again "much excited" and told Mr. Gass that it was a fraud (of which he offered no proof) and he would get into trouble with it and urged him to return it to the former owner. Mr. Gass was somewhat disturbed and thought of taking it back but I told him I would take the responsibility of holding it for further inquiry. I accordingly received contributions from members and through Mr. Gass settled with the man from whom he obtained it. My communication of this to the Academy appears in the minutes on page 274. Secretary's Book. "*Saturated with Grease*" Dr. R. D. Myers, who broke the pipe and who then examined the stone very carefully with [a] magnifying glass, stated to me last spring, and still states, that it was evidently not so.
>
> I have never detected a smell of linseed oil or other grease about the elephant pipes, either of them. I have never heard members say that they did. I have shown the pipes to many—perhaps hundreds —of visitors, many have examined them critically and sometimes suspiciously, have smelled of them and scrutinized them in every way and I never heard one speak of any smell about them, except a faint smell of tobacco in the larger one.
>
> Two of the pipes in the [display] case had a smell resembling that of linseed oil, or, as it was remarked by some one, "smelled like putty." To learn positively about the composition Mr. Gass and I broke one of them and found it of stone of a kind we have never met with elsewhere. Dr. Farquharson and I tried some of it from the inside, on red hot iron, but it produced no smoke and was not perceptibly affected. It has occurred to my mind that a person hearing these [words] spoken might have—perhaps unconsciously— transferred it in his memory, to the elephant pipes. . . .
>
> If however, it had been true that the said pipe was greasy after being about the house of the finder for several years, what would it signify? (Pratt 1886MS).

Another story circulating among members of the Academy at the time concerned the crystal found on top of the limestone tablet. Tiffany, in conversation, claimed it was from his own collection, had disappeared, and then mysteriously reappeared in the excavation (Bailey 1948:13). Although not telling us this story, Pratt refers to it in order to suggest it may be concocted. His remarks in full on this subject read:

> The first I ever heard of the remarks about the crystal was in 1885 (I think in conversation with yourself) [i.e. H. C. Fulton, chairman of the investigating committee] *over seven years* after the finding of the tablet. No remarks were made, as far as I ever heard, in the early days when the peculiarities of the crystal should have been fresh in his memory. *It is not mentioned in the letter to Norris.* (Pratt 1886MS).

Other points raised by the curator were equally impressive in influencing the committee. The Cook Farm mounds were in a very public place, the limestone tablet being found in a mound only a few rods from the road to Smith's limestone quarry. There were residences nearby:

> . . . hence it seems scarcely possible that a person could make an excavation of sufficient size and nearly four feet deep; bring a load of stones and build the "altar" and close all up and leave no traces —not even disturbing the sod [or] fence row covering a portion of it and through it all be unobserved by the many persons residing and working in the immediate vicinity and in full view of the place and frequently passing to and fro. (Ibid.)

Harrison's Report

Dated 2 January 1886, a two and one-half page handwritten statement was prepared by C. E. Harrison and given to the committee at their request. The Harrison summary is about his discovery of the limestone tablet in 1878 and the conduct of Tiffany. Since he had published the archaeological report, Harrison (1880:221-224) had nothing further to add to it:

> . . . and to this day, I have not heard with reference to this Limestone Tablet, any accusation or suggestion of fraud but what can be traced to Mr. Tiffany.
>
> I can further state that while I have often met and conversed with Mr. Tiffany—he has never once questioned me about the Tablet nor have I ever heard of any effort on his part to investigate or seek information additional to that which has been published. (Harrison 1886MS).

The impact of the vice-president's testimony was to clear himself, authenticate the relics, and lay the blame of the Academy's difficulties solely on Tiffany who had never sought Harrison's opinions or expressed his own to him.

Propounding Some Questions

The beginning of Dr. C. T. Lindley's difficulties with the Academy leadership had occurred a year or so earlier and broke into the open when he now began his private defense of Tiffany. In the Academy rooms at 3 P.M. on 4 March 1886, the committee of investigation met to hear testimony at a closed hearing. The unpublished minutes (Preston 1885-1886MS) state that President Putnam also attended. The major testimony was given by Dr. Lindley, who found he was well advised to avoid remarks that would bring a libel suit against him for damages. Consequently, he denied all knowledge, claimed he was misunderstood, and then gave his testimony in the form of rhetorical questions. Such were the circumlocutions forced by legal pressures from Putnam and C. E. Harrison.

> At his request, Dr. Lindley was allowed to read certain questions which he wished to propound, and read as follows:
> 1. Did the friends and members of D.A.N.S. [Davenport Academy of Natural Science] ever perpetrate an archaeological plant on A. S. Tiffany?
> 2. Did Chas. Harrison ever boast that he could make a 3000 year old arrow in 5 minutes?
> 3. Have stone and marble cutters ever made tablets of hieroglyphics and passed them off for genuine relics of antiquity?
> 4. Have any of the members of the D.A.N.S. ever attended a meeting of the A.A.A.S. [American Association for the Advancement of Science] and there referred to Mr. Tiffany in a disrespectful way as a man unworthy of attention, as a crank?
> 5. Did the Rev. Mr. Gass ever see any fraudulent curved-base pipe?
> 6. Did the Rev. Mr. Blumer [Gass' brother-in-law] ever have a, knowingly, fraudulent curved-base elephant pipe in his possession?
> Being asked as to his knowledge as to any of these questions, he refused to answer at this time.
> Being asked as to a statement that Mr. Graham's tools had been used in making the l.s. [limestone] tablet refused to explain at present. (Preston 1885-1886MS).

We may add Mr. Graham was the janitor of the Academy who was to testify before a subsequent and different committee, where he made the most startling revelations.

Harrison's Threat

At the same 4 March meeting where C. T. Lindley presented his questions, another man had previously appeared—the brother of C. E. Harrison. At Putnam's request, J. H. Harrison gave a statement that both

Harrisons would resign if Tiffany were continued as a member. This put the committee on notice that one side or the other would leave the group voluntarily or involuntarily. Since C. E. Harrison was becoming prominent in Academy affairs, his loss would be felt, and it would indeed look strange to the world if the principal discoverer of the limestone tablet disavowed all further connection with the Academy. Harrison was then first vice-president, a position which traditionally led to the office of president at the end of the year. He was, in fact, so well regarded that he was elected president in January 1887 over an unprecedented "opposition" ballot.

Consequently, we may not be surprised to learn that Harrison's statement of intent to withdraw had its desired effect. The committee moved and passed a motion to recommend expulsion of Tiffany without the alternative of censure. The Academy's general meeting would thus be without the option of keeping Tiffany, while chiding him for his stories. They would either have to expel him or find him innocent. Dr. Lindley's testimony had been of no help to Tiffany.

The threat of legal action kept Lindley and Tiffany from clearly presenting what they knew or suspected about the relics. Yet the committee seemingly felt satisfied, primarily because of the statement prepared by Pratt that such things as grease soaked elephant pipes and the crystal theory had no foundation.

The Tiffany committee had been pressured. At a subsequent public meeting Lindley hotly declared:

> The investigation began. One question was asked him. "Did you write any such letters?" He confessed to this one, and that stopped the investigation. No more was gone through with. The committee then disbanded to sign a paper that was to expel Mr. Tiffany, and not reprimand him as was represented to him. . . . The committee told Mr. Tiffany he was not going to be expelled. [They] told the friends and relatives of Mr. Tiffany that he was not to be expelled. Mr. Tiffany goes away. He leaves for the far west. In his absence after telling him he was not going to be expelled, what did the members of this institution do? . . . A meeting is held here. Then members are stopped on the street; members who attend meetings seldom. They are invited up to the Academy and told "You are wanted to sign a paper." (Lindley in McCowen 1886MSa).

The Expulsion of Tiffany

9

The stout defense of Tiffany by Thomas published in *Science* in late February made no impression whatever on the Davenport Academy. Possibly, the members read only Putnam. In March 1886, the committee reported to a regular meeting with twenty-eight members present that A. S. Tiffany should be expelled from membership. Those who may have doubted if the Putnam forces had the votes to carry off the expulsion were soon taught a lesson.

Dr. Lindley in the Meeting

Although there was some routine business, the purpose of the meeting was known to be a ratification of the conclusions and findings of the special committee on Tiffany. H. C. Fulton, its chairman, read the report, and the motion was made to expel Tiffany. The following record (McCowen 1886MS) is from the original handwritten copy; I have added some punctuation, changed abbreviations, deleted as indicated, and added an occasional connecting word. The transcript vividly conveys the heat of the discussion. The second vice-president, J. B. Phelps, presided.

> *Dr. Lindley* objected to the resolution. He thought the Academy could not afford to expel one of its "chartered" members. Mr. Tiffany had been an active and valuable member, and had on two different occasions saved the life of the Academy when it was gasping for breath. The beginning of the library was due to him. Mr. Tiffany had agreed to tell all he knew if criminal charges were not brought against him. He did not bring his charges before the Academy because past communications had been smothered. He had good reasons for making the charges he did. He knew frauds had been committed. He knew these tablets were frauds. Mr. Harrison had openly boasted of being able to make 3,000 year old arrow heads in five minutes—
>
> *Mr. Harrison* rose to a point of order.
>
> *Dr. Lindley:* "O, well, if you don't want the light let in on you, all right."
>
> *Chairman Phelps:* It is hardly necessary for Dr. Lindley to act as advocate for Mr. Tiffany. This matter has been thoroughly considered by the Committee and it is not necessary perhaps to debate it further.
>
> *Objections* were made by various members to cutting off debate.

Mr. Fulton called attention to the fact that Mr. Harrison's point of order was that Dr. Lindley was wandering from the point and indulging in personalities not connected with the subject under discussion and that the ruling of the Chair was meant to be in the same direction. No one objected to the fullest and freest debate of the questions properly before us.

The Chair so ruled.

On motion of Mr. Putnam, it was unanimously voted to allow Dr. Lindley to proceed.

Dr. Lindley said he was not here as an advocate for Mr. Tiffany, but thought he was not having fair treatment. Some of the most-respected citizens of this place believe Mr. Tiffany to be an ill-used old gentleman. Both officers and members have tried in every way to belittle him. Members have in the Association for the Advancement of Science called him an "old crank" and not entitled to any consideration. He would ask, had Mr. Tiffany any reasons for the course he pursued. He (Dr. Lindley) thought he had. Could he be expected to bring any charges in the Academy when his former communications had been carefully smothered? He thought not. As for this Committee, it was one-sided and did not want to reach the facts in the case. He (Dr. Lindley) was called before that Committee. He had 45 questions which would have thrown some light on this subject but they refused to hear them. Mr. Tiffany knew frauds had been committed but when threatened with a suit for libel if he told what he knew, of course he refused to do it. Mr. Tiffany is not alone in this. Some of the most respected members of this Academy believe these tablets to be a fraud. Mr. Tiffany *knew* curved-base pipes had been made in the Academy; that Mr. Harrison had made fraudulent tablets and passed them off as genuine.

The Academy is yearly losing in membership and we will take a wrong step and damage ourselves if we expel this old gentleman especially when he is not present to defend himself. This Academy owes an apology to Mr. Tiffany instead of a vote of expulsion.

Mr. Pilsbry called attention to the fact that Mr. Tiffany had had ample opportunity to make any defense he chose before the Committee.

On motion of Mr. Putnam it was unanimously voted to allow Dr. Lindley to read his 45 questions.

After some hesitation, *Dr. Lindley* said they were pertinent to the subject—but he thought he would not read them. It did not seem to be the proper time. He wished another Committee appointed who would be just and honest and would take into consideration all the facts in the case which ought to be investigated. This has got to be done sooner or later and when this Committee is appointed he would lay his questions before them.

Dr. Hazen said he did not rise as a champion of Mr. Tiffany nor of his conduct. Five members of this Academy, honorable men, chief members of the Academy, had carefully and thoroughly considered the question. Undoubtedly, their conclusions were sound and entitled to credence. Yet he personally had a good deal of sympathy for Mr. Tiffany. He had been a prominent member ever since the beginning. He had by personal solicitation collected from the citizens the first $300 which commenced our library, and he had been active in many ways in building up the Academy. He may be peculiar in many ways, eccentric. He may have been honest in his beliefs in regard to this matter—but mistaken. We think he *was* mistaken.

The Committee have not examined into the genuineness of the tablets but that is involved and ought to be considered. We ought to think well before tossing out an old man who has done so much. It ought to be very plain why we take such a step. I have a good deal of sympathy for Mr. Tiffany; there are many genuine, good things about him.

I think this resolution for expulsion is going to pass and I must say I think it ought to pass, but I don't think the resolution is plain enough. It ought to state more clearly that Mr. Tiffany's conduct is the point at issue and not the genuineness of the tablets or his doubting their genuineness.

The genuineness of the tablets is yet an open question, and we should always be ready to give a hearing to any honest argument or any competent testimony. All that we can claim is that the find was a genuine find made in good faith by the members of this Academy engaged in the search. Further than that we cannot say. . . .

Mr. Holmes said he had had little previous knowledge of this affair and was greatly surprised at what he had heard here this evening. It seemed from what had been said, that Mr. Tiffany being a member of the Academy was using his position from within to furnish the enemies of the institution with ammunition for its destruction. It seems he is making open statements to the world derogatory to its character and standing, is calling in question the integrity and honor of its members and then refuses to give the reasons for his belief or to bring forward the proof, which he says he has, in support of his statements. The defense attempted here for Mr. Tiffany is a charge against the good faith of the Committee and fresh charges against other members. If he thought this Academy so unjust, unfair and unscrupulous as we have heard this evening he should want to withdraw at once. He should not want to have anything to do with such a set of men.

Again, the right of the Academy to protect itself is challenged. He had not known much of this matter before, but it needed no other education than he had received on this occasion to make it clear that from the evidence offered here this evening the issue is a square one and one which must be promptly met.

Dr. Parry said no one was more reluctant than he to take measures against Mr. Tiffany. He had been on friendly terms with him for many years and had respect for what was true in the man. He was very loth to take any action which might seem hasty and as Mr. Tiffany was not present to speak for himself, he moved that action be postponed.

Mr. Kracke wished, if this motion prevailed, to add to it that Mr. Tiffany be notified to put in an appearance and defend himself.

Mr. Fulton called attention to the fact that this matter had *not* been hastily acted upon. It had been under consideration for *three months*. He had personally informed Mr. Tiffany that the report would be offered at this meeting. He had also notified Mr. Tiffany's attorney of the fact. The matter was well understood in all quarters.

Mr. Fulton regretted to the utmost that he had, after giving the most careful and thorough attention to this matter, found it his duty to sign the report as given by the Committee. There was no escaping the conclusion that in this case, heroic treatment was necessary and in his opinion now was the time. He was opposed to any postponement unless it could be shown wherein anything was to be gained by it.

Prof. Call hoped the motion would not prevail as it cast an imputation on the Committee.

Motion to postpone lost by unanimous vote. . . .

Mr. Thompson said that point had been very clearly kept in view throughout all this investigation and he thought it was clearly expressed in the findings of the Committee. Mr. Tiffany, his attorney, and his friends had continually tried to divert them from the main point, which was *Mr. Tiffany's* conduct. The argument offered that he should not be dealt with because he had once worked with the Academy and helped build it up was no argument at all, but rather an aggravation of his offense. The greater his activity in the past, the more reprehensible his conduct now.

Mr. Judy wished information in regard to the matter of expressing doubts of the genuineness of any relics first to the Academy; and asked if it was the sense of the members that, for example, he could not be allowed to write a private letter to a friend giving an adverse opinion of anything in the collection without first submitting such doubts to the Academy.

Prof. Call said that writing a letter, even if to a personal friend, who was to be an employee of a government Bureau, to be presented to the head of the Bureau and used in scientific circles to our prejudice was a very different affair from such a letter as contemplated in Mr. Judy's remarks.

Mr. Fulton thought the purport of his resolution was misapprehended but with the consent of his second he would strike out the wording objected to, which he accordingly did.

Mr. Judy withdrew his substitute, as with this change, Mr. Fulton's resolution met his approval.

Dr. Hazen's substitute lost.

Prof. Call seconded the original resolution as amended.

The motion being put seemed carried by a large majority. Dr. Parry calling for the yeas and nays, the vote stood as follows: [Aye 25, No 2]. . . .

Dr. Preston called attention to the statements made by Dr. Lindley in his speech in defense of Mr. Tiffany and thought they demanded notice.

Dr. Hazen thought no attention ought to be paid to anything said in the heat of debate.

Dr. Preston said these things had been said not only here and now, but also at other times and to various and sundry persons. Dr. Lindley had openly called in question the honesty and integrity of our Curator and had charged fraud upon other members. He thought we could not afford to ignore such statements and ought not wait.

Dr. Lindley said he wanted a committee appointed but hoped it would be a just and honest one that would be fair in its action, and one authorized to consider the whole question at issue. . . .

Dr. Lindley desired to have G. W. French on the Committee, and his name was willingly accepted by the mover.

There being some further desultory talk as to what had been said, *Mr. J. H. Harrison* protested against any further consideration of the subject. It had been referred to a Committee and the proper place now for these questions to come up was before this Committee. (McCowen 1886MS).

The Outcome

The vote of expulsion and the creation of yet another committee to investigate Lindley were a dramatic indication of Putnam's labors to shut off further discussion. In one letter to the chairman of the new committee, Putnam wrote, "this miserable business should be disposed of at the earliest moment practicable" and in another he wrote that Lindley's accusations were of "minor importance."

The membership did not have enough evidence from Lindley, but only his unsupported word. A number of members now felt that a new committee would be more thorough.

Suppression of Evidence

IO

Lindley met with the newly formed investigating committee which heard lengthy and embittered testimony, charges, and countercharges. At the end of the hearings, the committee suppressed the evidence. I presume they felt they had no alternative. To bring it all out in the open would have destroyed the Academy as a social group. It had already died as a research organization.

Disturbing Peace and Harmony

The April report was received from the committee investigating Lindley and in May 1885, with 37 members present, it was resolved that Dr. Clarence T. Lindley be expelled from the membership and his name struck from the roll. The reasons given were his unfounded charges, his hostility to the Academy, and his persisting in disturbing its peace and harmony; among other findings, the committee decided that retention of his membership would injure the standing of the Academy in the community (PDANS 5:222). Lindley refused to withdraw from the room during the discussion and vote, which incidentally was 36 to 0, for no one dared to protest further, and face disgrace and investigation in their own community, in addition to civil charges. A report of the committee was published in the *Proceedings*. Lindley had said:

1. That curved base pipes were made in the Academy;
2. That people about town know it;
3. That Mr. Pratt [the curator] knows all about it;
4. He (Lindley) not only knew that they were made, but had seen them made;
5. Mr. Tiffany had good reasons for his conduct, he knew the tablets were frauds, and that other frauds were committed;
6. He is not alone in this belief; it is shared by some of the most respected members of the Academy;
7. Mr. Harrison has made fraudulent tablets, and passed them off as genuine;
8. Mr. Pratt is dishonest in that if he should pack his (Lindley's) collection, he would drop out and leave behind the most valuable specimens;
9. The Committee on Tiffany's conduct did not want to reach the facts in the case, and were neither just nor fair in their action;

> 10. There are "goings on" at the Academy which he is going to throw
> light upon. He is going to see that every scientist in Europe hears
> of these things, and every time they are smoothed over he is
> going to "boom it up again."

> Your committee beg to report that, after a full examination, they
> find the charges made by Dr. Lindley not sustained. Lindley de-
> nied having uttered No. 7. (PDANS 5:221-223).

There is a mass of unpublished testimony in the files of the case.
From a letter Putnam wrote at the outset of Lindley's investigation we
find that the charges he reputedly made, subsequently published in
the *Proceedings,* were abbreviated. For example, charge 1 "that curved
base pipes were made in the Academy", and charge 2 that people
about town "know it" (Ibid.) really read as follows in manuscript:

> *First:* Curved base pipes have been made in the Academy. If people
> in town knew how many, their eyes would be opened.
> *Second:* People all about town know that bogus relics have been
> manufactured in the Academy. (Phelps 1886MS).

The other charges also vary somewhat from manuscript to finally
printed copy. The manuscript version contains an eleventh charge.
"There is a plot or conspiracy to injure him." (Ibid.). The manuscript
minutes together with sworn statements, depositions, and correspondence are filed under the committee chairman, J. B. Phelps.

The Janitor's Elephant

Lindley met with the committee in the Academy rooms on the after-
noon of Thursday, 22 May. By arrangement, he called the janitor to the
stand to testify. Although not a trial by law, to the participants, this
was a courtroom drama. The following testimony, excerpted from the
minutes, centers on platform pipes made by the janitor, John Graham:

> Lindley: You have been janitor here several years?
> Graham: Yes.
> Question: [You] have not been talked to in regard to certain
> charges except today?
> Reply: No.
> Question: Did you get pieces of stone and make curved base pipes?
> Reply: Yes.
> Question: Where did you make them?
> Reply: Made one at home. Elephant pipe. Nearly like one here at
> the Academy.
> Question: Did you not do some of your work here?
> Reply: No—except possibly to make hole larger for stem.

Question: Did you not block it out here?

Reply: No—may have broken off corners of a piece of stone here.

Question: What became of the pipe?

Reply: Had same at the Academy. Mr. Pratt and Mr. Bloomer saw it. I smoked it.

Question: What about other pipes you made?

Reply: Made four pipes altogether. Did not make any of them here. Might have made hole for stem larger here at the Academy.

Question: Do you remember the Bear pipe?

Reply: Yes. Never finished it. Had one called Seal pipe—

Question: You remember about curved base pipes!

Reply: Yes, the elephant pipe. Mr. Pratt, Mr. Bloomer, Mr. Gass all saw it. Mr. Bloomer took it. Have not seen it since.

Question: Are any pipes here represented? (Shows cuts) Curved base pipes?

Reply: No. Might be slight curve near the end. The Elephant pipe was curved. Took the block of stone from here to make the Elephant pipe.

Question by Committee: Did you ever pass off any pipe or pipes you made as mound-builder relics?

Reply: No.

Question by Committee: Did you ever know of any such relics being passed off as genuine?

Reply: No. (Phelps 1886MS).

Three drawings are pinned to the handwritten transcript. They portray three platform effigy pipes—a seal, a human foot, and a human head (plate 18). The handwritten caption on each says, "Pipe made by Jn. Graham." The elephant pipe is not present on the drawings. These may be the "cuts" shown by Lindley, or he might have shown Graham illustrations from the *Proceedings*.

Graham, as a witness, clearly hedged—promptly saying no, modified by a statement that carried a yes response. This equivocation is important when seeking to trace the history of the elephant found by Blumer in the Louisa County mound. Despite Graham's statement to the committee that he had no knowledge of fraudulent relics, he had made an elephant like the *one* in the Academy collection. But in 1880 there were *two*. The copy was last seen in the hands of Blumer in company with his brother-in-law Gass. I strongly suspect John Graham's elephant, partially made in the basement, is the specimen illustrated in plate 5.1.

Lindley (1886MS) presented a brief sworn statement, notarized, to the committee. In it, he states, "that between the first day of January 1880 and the first day of January 1885 I have seen curved base pipes in the process of manufacture in the building owned and occupied by the Davenport Academy of Science. And further, affiant saith not." January 1880, the beginning date of Academy pipe manufacture, fits with the second elephant discovery later in the same year. Lindley, the "affiant," a legal term for one who makes an affidavit, was cautious and did not draw the net tighter.

Pratt's Emotional Stability

As a practicing physician, Dr. Lindley seems to have suspected that all was not well with Curator Pratt. He consequently began a curious line of questioning, which his reluctant witnesses, the janitor and the janitor's wife, did their best to evade.

> Lindley: Have you ever seen Mr. Pratt in this institution?
> Graham: Yes often—
> Question: Have you seen Mr. Pratt in a passion, throw books around, etc.?
> Reply: Yes, we all do that at times.
> Question: Has he used profane language often?
> Reply: No, not often. Might have said d——n it, or something like that—
> Question: Does he get excited, throw books and papers!
> Reply: Not often. Possibly may have thrown books or papers off the table. Has some passions. Did not always control himself—
> Question: Has he slammed doors etc. when he lost his temper?
> Reply: Can't recollect [to] mind. Slams doors sometimes. Bolt was out once and [he] broke bolt or lock.
> Question: Did he lose his temper?
> Reply: Yes, was often tried. I often tried his temper. Could see he was irritated sometimes. (Phelps 1886MS).

Dr. Lindley later in the transcript attempted to get further information from the janitor's wife, calling Rachel Graham to the stand:

> Lindley: You are doorkeeper here?
> Rachel Graham: Yes. . . .
> Question: Have [you] seen Mr. Pratt about the Academy, have you seen him excited and throw things?
> Reply: Yes—a paper or something like that—
> Question: Did you see him in temper so as to be afraid of him?
> Reply: No—(Ibid.).

The doctor stopped this line of questioning when Rachel Graham replied negatively. She had not been afraid, and so Pratt's emotional stability was upheld. The curator, Putnam's right-hand man, did seem to have an extraordinarily high temper for a man in his sixties.

According to Pratt's (1887MS) own complaints on this testimony, Lindley had "endeavored to prove by Graham and Rachel that I was in the habit of 'frequently, *very* frequently' getting into an ungovernable rage, grossly profane, slamming doors and throwing things around and wrecking things generally: so absolutely losing all control of myself as to be 'not responsible for my actions.' His witnesses disclaimed knowledge of any such conduct on my part. Lindley said '*I have seen it dozens and dozens of times.*' This was in presence of all the above named persons [the committee members]." Pratt told this incident along with others to show Lindley was a liar.

Attacks on the Doctor

The Grahams' testimony made the curator look foolish and the Academy itself seem vaguely preposterous. Harrison, Pratt, Putnam, and others counterattacked. They aimed at showing Lindley to be dishonest, untrustworthy, and a crank. There is a great deal of manuscript evidence resulting from these charges, and a summary of some parts of it becomes relevant when evaluating the Academy as a scientific organization.

It comes as a surprise to learn that Dr. Lindley had been practicing medicine in the Academy itself. According to Lindley, "the trustees requested me to practice here." Charles Harrison finally ordered the doorkeeper, Rachel Graham, to inform Lindley's patients that he did not have an office in the Academy. This had angered the doctor, who maintained Mrs. Putnam was behind the removal because she did not like his patients: "Mrs. Putnam said they were not high toned enough to come here." (Phelps 1886MS).

According to a formal statement to the committee by Pratt, attached to the Preston manuscript, Lindley was the only member of the Academy he knew who might be making fraudulent relics. Pratt said he had no doubt about any of the archaeological specimens in the Academy. There was, however, an exception. "C. T. Lindley has rechipped broken flint implements, whether passed off by him as entirely of original Indian work or not I do not know: and, I have not examined the specimens in his collection and do not know as to the genuineness or history of them." (Pratt 8 April MS in Phelps 1886MS). Lindley never denied he chipped flint.

In the early years, the Academy provided storage space for the private collections of its members. Gass gave his finds to the Academy, but

Lindley did not, insisting that this storage service should be continued. This brought Lindley into conflict with Mrs. Putnam who said somewhat publicly, "When my husband gets to be president [your] collection will have to come out." In January 1886, Pratt took the cue and hired Martin Woods and Company to haul Lindley's collection away, to be redeemed upon payment of cartage and storage. Pratt, a compulsive saver, preserved the receipt.

Several years later, after the Tiffany and Lindley affair was closed, Pratt was still writing memos (to himself) about their disreputable conduct. One of these, apparently dated 1889, is a rather lengthy manuscript proving that Lindley's collection was not destroyed in a fire in 1887 and consequently he should not receive $3,000 compensation. It had been stored in the State Orphan's Home at the time of the fire, and a state claim was filed for damages (Senate File 243 Claims, 1889).

Lindley and his opponents wrangled over many other of the charges before the committee. The committee report that Lindley was guilty of misconduct was sustained by the membership at the May general meeting with only one negative vote. The unpublished minutes of the general meeting are attributed to Dr. Jennie McCowen (1886MSa) but are signed Jennie Warrick and are not in McCowen's handwriting.

Remarks in the May Meeting

From the minutes, it appears that not one member defended Lindley. A few of the statements illustrate the outspoken debate. Professor Sheldon claimed, "You can see by the report which has been made that not one of the charges was sustained. Not a particle of truth was found. I have much confidence in this committee in following up each and every point. . . ." In a lengthy rejoinder, Lindley replied:

> I do not know if I can make it as plain as I ought to; I know that Mr. Tiffany had made certain relics in the basement of the Academy and my speech had reference to the relics that the janitor made in the cellar. So far as saying Mr. Pratt was engaged in making such things, I never intimated anything of the kind. Nothing whatever. (McCowen 1886MSa).

Holmes said in a rebuttal that "Dr. Lindley has taken a course that compels us in self-defense to expel him as a member and exclude him from further usefulness. . . . I believe him honest in the matter, though laboring under a great hallucination. . . . The action of Dr. Lindley threatens the life of the Academy. It certainly does . . . we are called forgers, liars and perpetrators of iniquity, manufacturers of antique works. . . . When insinuations and denunciations of this sort are brought against us, I would acknowledge no private feelings whatever in the effort to free ourselves."

Finally, Professor Sheldon summarized the feelings of the assembly when he moved to close off debate. Croker had said:

> This is a matter of great importance. Some parties think it best to offer Dr. Lindley one more chance to free himself, so that he cannot say in the future that he was not having any chance.

Professor Sheldon replied:

> I should truly second that motion if Dr. Lindley has something new to offer. Something wherein he does not propose to make any charges against the Society. It is clear to me that Dr. Lindley should have no grounds for complaint. The Dr. has taken more time than all the rest together, and the last time, the time occupied was such that the chairman was unable to attend to unfinished business. Nothing more can be said further, and I move that the business of the evening be completed. (Ibid.).

Lindley's Hallucination

The proceedings have an eerie ring to them. Lindley could say no more and he had substantiated a number if not most of his charges. It was not the "hallucination," that Holmes and others believed it to be.

In the rhetorical questions he asked the Tiffany committee, he implicated Gass and Blumer with possession of a fraudulent elephant pipe, confirmed by the later testimony of the janitor. He claimed relics were made in the basement, and this was sustained. He claimed Pratt had seen them, and again the janitor supported him, although reluctantly. The Tiffany committee, by refusing to consider the question of genuineness of specimens, had backed off from reaching the facts of the case.

Lindley and Tiffany now embarked on a plan of revenge. People around town did in fact know about the manufacture of relics. The two expelled members began quietly to mend their forces, and soon the Academy was undergoing rapid expansion in membership as their friends joined. The bid was being secretly made to overthrow Putnam and his regulars at the next election. Putnam had not heard the last from the enraged physician.

Secret Inquiries

II

Mr. A. F. Berlin (1886a) wrote a complaint in the *American Antiquarian* that Putnam threatened libel against all who questioned the Gass discoveries. The threat is tempered in the publication, both in the Academy's own *Proceedings* and in various rejoinders ·in the journals. Was Berlin a reliable witness, or was he exaggerating to gain sympathy? Those unpublished documents that are still available demonstrate conclusively that Putnam was making private inquiries through attorneys in various parts of the country, suggesting libel suits, and obtaining personal information to vindicate the elephant pipes and inscribed tablets. His attempts represent a unique aspect of the case.

In defense of Putnam's motives, but not his actions, he was firmly and totally committed to the validity of the archaeology and the enormous import of the relics. The men who found them were honest. If these "undoubted facts" were true, and he "knew" them to be so, then those who were attacking the relics had ulterior motives. It was a conspiracy emanating from Washington, possibly through jealousy, but it was obviously well financed, since so many agents of the conspiracy were laboring to destroy the Academy. Yet such a conspiracy with so many people had a basic weakness by weight of numbers. Some of them would be easy to expose through libel suits and, this done, the whole fabric of the plot would shred, leaving the principal plotters exposed. It is necessary to understand Putnam's point of view in order to place the following discussion of the documents in their proper perspective.

A Friend of Justice

In an envelope still preserved with the Tiffany case files, there is a remarkable note. The envelope, postmarked 4 P.M., 22 January 1886, Washington, D.C., is addressed to Putnam and is stamped received 29 January. It is addressed in a slightly shaky, smudged, but upright flourished script in brown ink. Inside, on cheap unlined paper lacking a watermark, and written in the same hand, in pencil, is the undated note. It is brief, but poisonous. Without an address or salutation and in its entirety it reads:

Are you aware that Powell has *bought* Peet up with a salary? That

is the "true inwardness" of his "change of heart"—Let your Congress-
man or some friend in Washington see into it, and keep this letter a
secret—burn it, in fact,

A Friend of Justice.

This note (Anonymous 1886MS) is in handwriting that does not match
any in the collection of correspondence. It served, we may presume, its
purpose. By this time, Putnam (1885) had circulated the first version
of *Elephant Pipes and Inscribed Tablets,* and Peet, in November 1885
had published his first doubts based on his knowledge of the Gass-
Stevens correspondence. Putnam's repeated allusions to the conspiracy
emanating from Powell's Bureau of Ethnology were a matter of record.
That this note was saved, rather than burned, as the sender requested,
places it in some possible importance. I don't know how anonymous
it was to Putnam, for the quotation marks suggest a reply to a previous
query. In any event, confidential inquiries were to follow.

Peet's Character

With growing suspicion, Putnam decided it was now necessary to investigate the Reverend Stephen Peet of the *American Antiquarian* to
find out if the latter's doubts about the unique relics could be financially linked with the Bureau of Ethnology. Peet lived in Clinton, Wisconsin. Putnam, therefore, sent off two letters to Mr. William Jones
(whose envelope identifies him as "Superintendent"), an attorney
resident in the town who replied in nearly illegible handwriting.

> Mr. Peet is highly resp'ct'd in this community. My personal estimate
> of him is that he is a gentleman of integrity & high character.
>
> I greatly regret the intelligence you communicate. I hope it may
> turn out that the exact facts do not warrant your indictment of him.
>
> As to his goods moneys rentals. If he has of these any thing
> where-with-al to satisfy an execution, I know nothing thereof, but
> my belief is that such an instrument would have to be returned
> "De bonis non."
>
> As to the "Magazine," you probably are yourself aware that his
> connection therewith commits in no wise to a leviable interest.
>
> As to my participating with you in a prosecution of the "Case".
> My relations with him are such that I must be excused. I am under
> no obligations to him which import me to refuse, am not a member
> of *his* church—of any church, for that matter—but the rest of the
> folks are, & for that reason I pray you excuse me. (Jones 1886MS).

A *Hint of Blackmail*

There is a gap in the correspondence and no further word was received from Jones that we know of, but Putnam was not content with the strong recommendation of Peet he had received. In the Peet correspondence, we find the following letter dated 27 April 1886, addressed to C. E. Putnam:

> Your various communications have been received. I have felt under no particular obligations to answer them. In the first place, you seem to have undertaken to get at me through the courts, and have even come to members of my own congregation to make me trouble.
>
> Second, you threaten to publish all the correspondence, private and personal, as well as that which is of public interest.
>
> Third, there is no reason why you should act as a medium between the members of your Society and the Antiquarian. The Secretary has already done that.
>
> Fourth, Mr. Gass has the right to be heard, but he will be heard in his own name and not through a lawyer who is seeking to catch me and make me trouble.
>
> Fifth, there is no advantage to science arising from a personal squabble between me and the President of the Davenport Academy. The public has no interest in it, we are neither of us of enough importance for that.
>
> Sixth, the defense of the Society does not require any publication or any litigation [but] if you are anxious for the latter you should have attacked Mr. Henshaw and the Bureau and not me. Mr. Gass has a right to defend himself. If he wants to send me a communication, he can send it in German. I will have it translated and then decide whether I will publish it or not. The tone of his letter will probably influence the public mind more than any specific arguments—He should be left to himself to give his own tone to it. I will not promise beforehands to publish any thing and I reserve to myself the right to edit my magazine in my own way. This thing is certain, that personal abuse will not appear in the pages, if I can help it. I have already cut out from letters, language of that kind and have rejected letters. The only communication which contained expletives and personalities is the one which I published for the Secretary of your Society. (Peet 1886MS).

The Secretary of the Society was Pratt who published the attack in Peet's own journal (1886), as described in Chapter Seven "The Curator Enters the Fray."

The letter from Peet to Putnam reveals the most depressing aspects of the attorney's personality. He had evidently gone beyond what must have been the two most strongly worded inquiries to Jones in Clinton,

Wisconsin. Peet was vulnerable. In this modern day of scholarly journals, we are perhaps unaware of the difficulty such ventures had in this country a century ago. Peet ran his journal singlehandedly and supported himself by preaching. By "coming to members of my own congregation to make me trouble," Putnam was cutting into Peet's sole source of economic support. There may already have been some dissatisfaction from a local level because of the time required in professional editing, writing, correspondence, soliciting articles, and acting as circulation manager as well. Putnam saw a chance to get at Peet effectively through the congregation, and indeed Peet moved both himself and the *Antiquarian* to Mendon, Illinois, in the fall of 1887. Since that town currently has a population of about 800, we may imagine the ministerial duties were neither well recompensed nor prestigious a century ago.

The threat to publish Peet's "private and personal" correspondence is a puzzle, since the only communications in the file are routine letters between Peet, Putnam, and Pratt. I don't know what is involved here; whether Putnam purchased or otherwise obtained some letters that no longer survive, but it is a matter having overtones of blackmail. Putnam did not make idle threats. Questioning the genuineness of the tablets and elephant pipes was a serious affair, and Peet had compounded his offense against the Academy in substantiating the charges by publishing Gass' strange dealings with the Oregon relic trader, Stevens.

Whatever is involved in the persecution of the Reverend Stephen Peet for publishing the Berlin article and the Gass-Stevens correspondence, we may be certain it was not archaeology. Putnam had developed suspicions of such depth and intensity, and planned such far-ranging attacks, that if any judgment is to be made of his character it is to suggest that he might have benefited from medical treatment for symptoms of paranoia.

Pennsylvania Lawyers

In an effort to find out about Berlin whom he suspected of the basest motives in publishing the Gass-Stevens correspondence, Putnam wrote to the legal firm of R. E. Wright's Sons, Allentown, Pennsylvania. He found them eager to do business. His letter of 12 March 1886 reached them on 15 March, was answered and postmarked the same day, and was stamped received in Davenport on 17 March. They replied:

Mr. A. F. Berlin is a young man whose only business has been that of salesman, though I believe he does have a collection of objects that indicate that his mind is affected with feeble aspirations towards thoughts "scientific."

He is respectable as the world goes but narrow minded, bigoted and with all the self-assurance that usually comes with ignorance.

He is a man of limited means however and owns no property that we know of.

There is nothing to prevent our being concerned against him in litigation. (Wright 1886MS).

Oregon Lawyers Respond

Stevens, who engaged in the correspondence with Gass and complained to Berlin about receiving fraudulent relics, was another man in the "plot to attack the Academy," and Putnam thought he would bear watching. Accordingly, he dispatched a letter to Oregon City, Oregon, addressed to C. D. and D. C. Latourette, Attorneys at Law. Sent 12 March 1886, the letter was answered almost immediately:

Yours of the 12" inst. came to hand yesterday—It was in reference to one H. C. Stevens R. R. agt. & ck.—Yes, we know the man well. He is financially responsible. He has the reputation of being *ordinarily* truthful and honest—He has some real estate—and some money at interest, and is probably worth from $5,000 to $7,000 dollars—

If desired we could act with you in libel suit against him if you have a good case. (Latourette 1886MS).

A Geological Plot Against the Academy

The conspiracy theme, of plotters discrediting the Academy, took strange forms and seems to have been widely held by local members. For example, there is a note from a former member, E. W. Claypole of Akron, Ohio, addressed to Pratt, and dated 6 February 1886. It refers to previous correspondence about *a geological fraud* that adds to the complexity of Academy affairs:

Dear Mr. Pratt . . . I am afraid you are right in regard to those pseudo-fossils and that they were a trap laid by somebody for the Academy. I wish however you would set the whole thing at rest for ever by analysing the material which I am confident you will find to be Plaster of Paris. As to its being a Niagara fossil I was quite certain that was not the case. That it was a make-up also I was equally sure, but of what I could not say. The mismatching of the valves satisfied me on this point. . . . I feel very glad you have never committed yourselves to it in any way for it would have hurt you much in the controversy about the elephant pipes. It is very unpleasant to have such disputes in a scientific society and never does any good. But I do not see how you could have avoided this nor do I see what motive T. can have in trying to throw discredit on the Academy unless it be on account of some grudge which he feels. (Claypole 1886MS).

Last Inquiries and the Opposition Ticket

Putnam could not rest from his labors. He was puzzled by the 1886 request of Dr. Lindley to have Mr. George W. French on his investigation committee. Although the committee had voted to recommend expulsion, Putnam felt that the loyalty of Mr. French should be examined. The issue was raised by a challenge to the leadership of the Academy. Although it failed, there was an "opposition ticket" at the January 1887 election, when Putnam retired as President and Mr. C. E. Harrison succeeded him. "Mr. Harrison has just handed me a *Rock Island Argus* containing a very inaccurate account of our meeting which gives occasion for correction," Putnam wrote Pratt on 31 January 1887. He also asked for detailed information:

> *1st* What offices has Hon. Geo. H. French filled in the Academy? and when? Was he an elected president and declined? and if so when? Was he ever elected to any other office which he declined? if so when? Has he attended the meetings of the Acadmy, and if not when did he cease to do so?
> *2nd* Geo. W. French (the son) was formerly I think a member, but declined to pay his dues, and subsequently I think was re-elected. I would like the *dates* and *facts?* Do the records show any attendance of this same man upon our meetings?
> *3rd* As to Tiffany and Lindley, I wish the dates of their expulsion, the names of the members of the committees who investigated same, the *number* of members present at their expulsion and the respective votes thereon & will if can state each separately.
> *4th* I wish the *dates* when the persons whose names appear on the "opposition ticket" were elected to membership in the Academy, & when recommended, and how many meetings they had attended previous to becoming candidates for the office therein. (Putnam 1887MS).

This was to be among the last of Putnam's inquiries into his world of schemers, plotters, and enemies both from within and without the Academy—

Tiffany and Lindley's Revenge

The sputtering questions Putnam asked of Pratt were answered in another memo and followed a fantastic attempt made by Tiffany and

Lindley to take over the Academy and throw out the Putnam leadership. The newspaper account was characteristically saved by Pratt to
show what a worthless fellow the doctor was:

> The *Argus* of last night mentioned the factional fight raging among
> members of the academy of science at Davenport, which includes
> many from this side of the river. The history of the difficulty is
> quite interesting. Nearly a year ago, shortly after the annual election
> of officers, which resulted in the choice of C. E. Putnam for presi-
> dent, two of the Davenport members, to whom the result of the
> election was not altogether satisfactory, made themselves so con-
> spicuous in denouncing the new officers that they were expelled
> from membership. During the past year the academy has ex-
> perienced a wonderful growth in membership; hardly a meeting has
> been held that applications were not made for initiation, and the
> society rather rejoiced than otherwise over its apparent prosperity.
>
> Suddenly, however, a bombshell was exploded, it revealed the
> reason for this unexplained growth, for back of it was seen the
> hands of the expelled members. They had adopted this underhand
> method of gaining the ascendancy by the votes of the new mem-
> bers, whose friends they were, and thus intruding themselves upon
> the society from which they had been expelled, and sounding the
> first notes of discord, which had not existed in the academy before.
>
> The discovery was made only a few weeks ago—but a short time
> before election. The members of the academy saw and realized the
> impending danger and saw too that in bringing out a full at-
> tendance on election night, the expelled members might be voted
> down. All the loyal members were notified and last night carriages
> were flying around as on occasion of a political election.
>
> The result of the annual election was the triumph of the academy,
> two to one, there being ninety-two members present out of whom
> the expelled members controlled thirty-one. Had not a full at-
> tendance been called out, however, the expelled members would
> probably have succeeded in their scheme. (*Rock Island Argus* 27
> January 1887).

The opposition to Putnam and Harrison was thorough. Pratt saved
one of their printed ballots, cut for tearing off the individual names
and putting the strips into the ballot box. Ordinarily, the attendance
at the annual meeting was about thirty, as it was in 1886 and 1888. By
bringing in that many dissidents, the opposition hoped to take the
1887 meeting by storm. Word had inevitably leaked out and the car-
riages hustling sixty elderly members to the meeting broke the revolt.
Putnam wrote a lengthy, bitter, partisan attack for the newspaper "in
the belief that many excellent members voted with the minority under
an entire misapprehension as to the true state of affairs." The factional
fight was waged by the two expelled members inspired by personal re-

sentment, men who had committed offenses of grave import. It "gives occasion for surprise that a movement so evidently revolutionary in its character should have enlisted in its support some of our most worthy citizens." Putnam termed Tiffany and Lindley malcontents, but nevertheless "cunning and audacious." They had circulated a petition among prominent businessmen, proposing names on the opposition ticket of men who rarely attended, were not equipped to run the Academy, and in two cases, had not even been consulted about having their names placed on the ballot. Among those proposed for trustee, Putnam was enraged to discover the name of Dr. Bowman, Dr. Lindley's medical partner. After a lengthy review of each of the twelve men on the opposition ticket, naming names and attendance records at Academy functions, he concluded that it was his duty to the Academy "to make public a plain statement of facts." (Putnam 1887MSa). The outspoken and one-sided writings of this lawyer were presented in a style of fulminating triumph, for Harrison had succeeded to the presidency and the opposition, put down, was not to reappear.

The End of the Amateur Contributor

The minutes and manuscripts of the Davenport association provide vivid examples of its nonscientific goals and methods and show up the weakness of the era of the amateur contributor. In all the torrents of words before committees and meetings, the striking fact emerges that none of the principals referred to the scientific publications of Thomas, Peet, and Berlin that were then current and provided such damning discussions of the elephants, the tablets, and their finders.

The Academy possessed many of the attributes of a social club. This raises the question, why didn't the two "disgraced" members and their supporters band together and found a rival academy? One reason was the growing obsolescence of the Academy type of scientific organization, centered in a small midwestern city and lacking professional leadership. A second and equally compelling reason for the disappearance of the Lindley faction was that very few Davenport citizens were interested in natural science and other fields. In its heyday, the Davenport Academy often had no more than four or five members attend the monthly meetings organized by "sections" in geology, history, natural history, or archaeology. In the history section, two members met fairly regularly and talked to each other about early Davenport memorabilia. In geology, three or more gathered together and heard talks on collections and rock outcrops. In the early 1880s, Jacob Gass' section on archaeology sometimes drew as few as two other members to hear his disquisitions on the mounds; a talk on two new plant species from southern California by Dr. Parry brought out four other members. Sometimes attendance was higher. Eighteen members turned out in the fall of 1879 to hear Dr. Lindley give "an interesting, popular paper on the boomerang." A glance at volume 3 of the *Proceedings,* covering the various meetings from 1879 through 1881, provided these examples of local involvement and activity.

An analysis of the membership lists at the end of 1881 provides an illusory picture of organizational health. The total of 434 members enrolled in the Academy included 230 in an honorary and corresponding group of nonresidents, many of them professional scientists who received the *Proceedings* but did not pay dues regularly, if at all. Of 204 residents, at least 8 were deceased at the time the list was compiled; wives, husbands, and sometimes older children were listed separately to reach the membership total, as one might do in listing church membership. For example, nine Putnams were life members and four Pratts were enrolled, including the curator, his wife, and his daughters, Miss Lucy and Miss Frankie Pratt. The list of separate surnames, excluding known deceased members, reduces the total to 143, most of them inactive. The Academy was locally considered a worthy cause, mildly prestigious, a learned association, an organization that prominent or prosperous citizens could support for three dollars a year. Among the membership, only 53 felt sufficiently involved to contribute to the building fund of 1877-1878 although a contribution of five dollars was sufficient for having one's name on the printed list of donors (PDANS 3:61). Of the membership, only 190 actually subscribed to receive volume 3, and the list included 120 Davenport residents, the majority of the remainder living in Iowa and Illinois communities.

The disgruntled minority could not organize another academy because there were no amateur scientists beyond a handful of elderly men most of whom were dead in the 1890s. For the most part, the local contributors to the *Proceedings* were dabblers, with important exceptions. The early volumes contained a stream of meeting notes, announcements, resolutions, and local members' scientific observations on a variety of topics, such as lightning phenomena, paleontological finds, or a discussion of the question whether rifle balls burn upon impact. Volume 5, covering the years from 1885 to 1889, is the last of this type of *Pro-*

ceedings. Volume 6 still contained minutes of meetings, but the scientific papers were contributed by professional scientists. In later volumes, even the minutes were discontinued, and with them local participation and the chance to see one's name in print. The series finally became an outlet for Ph.D. theses completed at The University of Iowa in natural history until the *Proceedings* themselves ceased publication after 1910. The great contention and factionalism of 1886 to 1887 had also marked the demise of the publications of the amateur contributor. By 1890, such articles were no longer considered of value or being submitted to the publication committee. While this was inevitable as scientific fields became more complex, the volcanic clash of personalities had hastened the trend within the Academy. As a scientific group, it had been living beyond its intellectual means.

Aftermath

12

In June 1887, the residence of Charles E. Putnam on his eighteen-acre estate "Woodlawn" burned to the ground. Although there was no loss of life, the fire destroyed a large portion of his library and all of his own and his deceased son's literary manuscripts. It was a bitter personal shock to him. He moved into a cottage on the grounds planning to rebuild. Six weeks later, he suddenly died at the age of sixty-three.

The Putnam family—there were seven surviving children—continued to take the greatest interest in the Academy and his wife served as president. The family, through endowments, provided for the survival of the Academy and its later development into the Davenport Public Museum. Putnam's remarkably successful business career and various intellectual interests are described in the *Proceedings* (PDANS 7:3-13).

In terms of the controversy, Putnam, as a lawyer, was accustomed to the exaggerated role of legal advocate in courtroom style, magnifying discrepancies and proliferating arguments. In consequence, the conflict had long since passed beyond the resolution of scientific problems. One of the unfortunate aspects of the case was the skill, personal magnetism, and convictions of the principal defender. Had he been less able, the controversy would have died, and the truth, we suspect, would have come out at the time. As this chapter will indicate, continued bitterness, errors, and confusion survived the death of Putnam and in no small measure became his legacy to science.

Servile Followers

In 1890, Major Powell wrote an article in a national literary magazine, *The Forum*, on the subject of "Prehistoric Man in America." With an oblique reference to his colleague Henshaw and the threats of Putnam, he remarked calmly:

> Not long ago a local society had in its possession two elephant pipes, the antiquity of which was questioned, in a passing sentence of an article, by one of the most skillful archaeologists of the country. Thereupon the society held meetings, and had their attorney make a careful investigation to see if the offending scientist could be successfully prosecuted for libel. And all this was in the interest of

science, the high antiquity of man, and the exaltation of the ancient
Mound-builders! (Powell 1890:493).

Powell's statements aroused a reprisal in *The Naturalist,* a monthly
publication of the Kansas City, Missouri, Academy of Sciences. The full
three columns of the front page and another two on a back page contained an article by Warren Watson entitled "Those Elephant Pipes
Again." In this article, Watson denounced Powell for knowingly publishing untrue remarks and falsehoods. The conclusions illustrate the
tenor of his remarks all too clearly:

> It is true these finds are unique and in this respect require great
> circumspection in their authentication; but this fact does not justify
> the brutal unfairness exhibited by Maj. Powell and his pseudo-
> archaeologist, Mr. Henshaw; especially when we consider that it
> is the money of the government and the prestige of official position
> that gives their attack a force and currency above that of mere
> personal opinion. If the power placed in Maj. Powell's hands is to
> be misused and prostituted to the furtherance of his own hobbies,
> instead of the interests of science, a concerted action should be taken
> by all interested in scientific pursuits, looking to an investigation
> by Congress into the policy, methods and expenditures of the
> Bureau, to the end that the liberal sums appropriated from the
> public funds in aid of ethnological inquiries may not be diverted to
> the exploitation of personal hobbies and the aggrandizement of
> servile followers. (Watson 1890).

Powell's "hobby" was encouraging his "servile followers," and particularly Cyrus Thomas, finally to resolve the mound builder question in
American archaeology.

A Note on Henshaw

The depth of feeling against Henry Wetherbee Henshaw, and the
general abuse he suffered for his generally correct remarks, are simply
beyond belief. Most of this is directly attributable to Putnam's defense
of the elephant pipes when he published the correspondence and first
journal reviews. It was this 1886 publication that was widely read by
men like Watson apparently unaware of the raging controversy and re-
buttals that had appeared in *Science* and elsewhere. To redress the
balance in some small measure, we may say the charges that Henshaw
was only an ornithologist and not qualified to judge archaeological
matters are not sustained. Henshaw was professionally able in anthropology, as his publications in linguistics, ethnology and archaeology
indicate. Henshaw's publications and contributions appeared in the

Annual Reports of the Bureau of Ethnology, the *American Anthropologist,* and the *American Antiquarian.* He was also engaged in assisting Powell in the latter's major works.

Powell Returns to the Mound Builder Problem

In 1894, the U.S. Bureau of Ethnology published its *Twelfth Annual Report,* containing an Administrative Report by the director, Major Powell, and a single 700-page monograph on "Mound Explorations" prepared by Cyrus Thomas. This monograph, developed over a decade, was a summation and elaboration of Cyrus Thomas' earlier articles and monographs. It concluded with an exact, detailed, and conclusive chapter on the mound builder question in American archaeology. Powell explained the need for the study in his introduction:

> It is difficult to exaggerate the prevalence of this romantic fallacy, or the force with which the hypothetic "lost races" had taken possession of the imaginations of men. For more than a century the ghosts of a vanished nation have ambuscaded in the vast solitudes of the continent, and the forest-covered mounds have been usually regarded as the mysterious sepulchers of its kings and nobles. It was an alluring conjecture that a powerful people, superior to the Indians, once occupied the valley of the Ohio and the Appalachian ranges, their empire stretching from Hudson bay to the Gulf, with its flanks on the western prairies and the eastern ocean; a people with a confederated government, a chief ruler, a great central capital, a highly developed religion, with homes and husbandry and advanced textile, fictile, and ductile arts, with a language, perhaps with letters, all swept away before an invasion of copperhued Huns from some unknown region of the earth, prior to the landing of Columbus. These hypothetic semicivilized autochthons, imagined to have been thus rudely exterminated or expelled, have been variously identified by ethnologists with the ancestors of the Aztecs or the Toltecs, the Mayas, the Colhuas, the Chichimecs, or the Pueblos, who have left no sign of their existence save the rude and feeble fortifications into which they fled from their foes, and the silent and obscure elevations in which their nobles found interment. . . .
>
> Now as these tumuli are unnumbered and may fairly be said to be innumerable, it is obviously impossible that every mound can be scientifically examined and a complete correlation and coordination thus established. If it can be shown that some of the mounds and some of the other antiquities of all the different types and classes were made by Indians, or even by people having the same habits, beliefs, and culture-status as the Indians, the inference is justifiable that all are the work of the same race or one closely allied in culture. In fact, such an inference from such data is ir-

resistible. Prof. Thomas has made, in the paper herewith presented, a comprehensive accumulation of these significant facts which seems to overwhelm all a priori theories of a "lost race" and to demonstrate inductively that all of these mounds were built by the people known to have built some of them or by other people of similar characteristics and of the same grade of culture. (Powell 1894: XLI-XLII, XLV).

The extensive monograph by Thomas on mound explorations, so highly praised by Powell's introduction, had a lengthy section on various theories of the mound builders. In reviewing and discarding faulty evidence, Thomas was forced to discuss once again the Davenport tablets. He reviewed the evidence in great detail and concluded:

A consideration of all the facts leads us, inevitably, to the conclusion that these relics are frauds: that is, they are modern productions made to deceive. It is by no means a pleasant task to present this subject to the public in what we believe to be its true light. It is proper, however, to add that the members of the Davenport Academy are, with the single exception named, so far as known, firm believers in the genuineness and authenticity of these finds. (Thomas 1894:642-643).

Cyrus Thomas, in referring to Tiffany as the sole disbeliever, was apparently unaware of the published *Proceedings*, volume 5, which had appeared one year earlier, in 1893. This volume contained the published version of the expulsion of Lindley and Tiffany in the year 1886. It was by now a minor matter. Equivocation was past, and the fraudulent nature of the tablets should have been accepted by everyone. On the national scene, this appears to have been the case. Locally, Putnam's legacy kept the matter in doubt until 1930.

Speeches to the Academy

In the Davenport Academy, the issue was closed with the expulsions and the breakup of the opposition group. The established leadership would brook no further inquiry. In 1892, James Thompson, president of the Academy, had used Putnam's published phrases in the annual address to the membership. Concerning the specimens, he said, "the genuineness . . . has been proven by honest and unimpeachable witnesses" and urged they be put on exhibit at the forthcoming Columbian Exposition in Chicago. It would "give visitors from all parts of the world a chance to see something that has made a little stir in the scientific world and now is only waiting, like the Rosetta Stone, for some

Marietta [*sic*] to decipher the story hidden in its hitherto undecipherable hieroglyphics." (Thompson 1892:306-307).

The theme of the unique relics was a main subject in the President's Address delivered the next year by Dr. W. L. Allen. His listeners scarcely needed to be told in 1893 that "natural pride in our city and its reputation should impel every citizen to familiarize himself with, and then show his children, the 'Davenport inscribed tablets' and the 'Davenport elephant pipes.'" (Allen 1893:317). He was reelected president. In the Annual Address of 1894, he cited the writings of Putnam and urged the Academy to "devote most of its time and work to this particular branch of archaeological research." (Allen 1894:330). Serving a third term when the final report of Powell and Thomas appeared in 1894, the president attacked it in his Annual Address of 1895, but it was so repetitious the publication committee declined to print it (PDANS 6:338).

Frederick Starr's Equivocations

During the 1890s, a reevaluation of Iowa archaeology was undertaken by Dr. Frederick Starr. At Coe College in Cedar Rapids, about 1886 or 1887, he taught the first course in anthropology in the state—one of the first examples of definite college instruction offered in this field. Thereafter, Starr became the first professor of anthropology at the University of Chicago and a founder of the American Anthropological Association (Ward 1903:7). Although primarily an ethnographer, he published on Iowa archaeology and was an active corresponding member of the Davenport Academy.

In order to give archaeological explorations more direction, he circulated a useful annotated bibliography in 1892, and in 1895 compiled a thorough survey of reported discoveries in 40 of Iowa's 99 counties. Both Starr's reports were published (1897) together with a circular on archaeological planning (1897b). Although he published a full bibliography on the controversy, he declined to take a stand (1897:111). In a detailed history of the Davenport Academy in *Popular Science*, describing the formation, contributions, and principal men associated with its development, the Reverend Mr. Gass is not mentioned, but among the various illustrations accompanying the article are the Hunting and Cremation Scene tablets. In the text, Starr says of the five unique relics:

> While this is not the proper place for discussing the authenticity

> of these specimens, it may not be out of place for the writer to say
> that to his judgment no substantial argument by the opposition
> demonstrates either the falsity of the specimens or fraud on the
> part of the academy. A careful examination of the objects themselves
> by a disinterested and impartial committee has never been made.
> Until it has been, every expression of opinion can only be personal.
> (Starr 1897a: 92-93).

He had, in short, disqualified himself, since one man is obviously not a
committee. Indeed he may have felt the effects of a full disclosure of
the Davenport Academy frauds by such a trusted corresponding member as himself might have been harmful to the continued life of the
organization:

> Just at this time of favorable financial condition came the attack
> upon the elephant pipes. Whether this was intended to harm the
> academy or not, it had that result. The society was already weak-
> ened by loss of active members. . . . Interested and self-sacrificing
> members remained, but they were not professional scientists. The
> attack surprised some, disgusted others, discouraged more. A few
> brave workers kept their hands on the work. Among them the
> curator [Pratt] was indefatigable. (Starr 1897a: 93-94).

The intimation that the attack might have been motivated by an intent
to harm the Academy was an unfortunate legacy inherited from Putnam.

The local scientific influence of Frederick Starr was considerable in
the first decade of the twentieth century. While teaching at Chicago,
he maintained his relationships with the Davenport Academy and interested investigators within Iowa. Despite considerable activity of
high quality in the first decade of the twentieth century, the unique
specimens were not reviewed.

Elephant Pipes

After the turn of the century, such marginal sources as the *History of
Scott County* proudly wrote of the victory of Putnam and the Academy
over the relic sharps in the Bureau of Ethnology. More important, a
few professionals were still giving qualified support to the elephants,
which were harder to abandon than the tablets.

The elephant pipes were an attractive nuisance, to use a legal phrase.
In 1886, Max Uhle published "Zwei prähistorische Elephantendarstell-
ungen aus Amerika" in the prestigious German publication *Zeitschrift
für Ethnologie*. In this article based on Putnam's version of the de-

fense, Uhle rejected Henshaw's arguments as poorly prepared and tended to accept the claim for genuineness. In America, Stephen Peet reversed his ground once again and supported the claims of the elephants, while maintaining the tablets were "doubtful." At first he regarded them as a plant after publishing the Gass-Stevens correspondence. (1886b:256). He accepted the view, however, that elephant extinction was recent and the version that Gass was not the primary discoverer of both pipes. Consequently, he was led to accept them as authentic artifacts in a discussion he republished repeatedly (1891:266, 1892:76, 1903:47). This cautious argument seemed hard to impeach at the time, for the substance of Lindley's remarks about the manufacture of pipes was buried in the manuscript minutes of the Academy archives.

Keyes to Antiquity

In 1920, Professor Charles Reuben Keyes read a paper entitled "Some Materials for the Study of Iowa Archaeology" to the Iowa Academy of Science. The superintendent of the State Historical Society, Benjamin Shambaugh, learning of the paper, published it the same year. This paper is little more than an expression of interest in Iowa archaeology, but it does mention some of the publications subsequent to Starr. This summary led the State Historical Society to appoint Keyes at the age of 51 to a part-time position as "Research Associate and Director of the Iowa Archaeological Survey," a position he held until his death in 1951 when the title was discontinued. He has sometimes been referred to as the State Archaeologist (see Petersen 1951:281), but this is incorrect, for that appointment was not created until 1959 when it was established at The University of Iowa as a Board of Regents appointment.

Keyes made substantial contributions to Iowa archaeology, which are mentioned more fully elsewhere (McKusick 1964). No injustice to him is intended, when I quote the following remarks he wrote in 1920 in the *Iowa Journal of History* when first starting his systematic research. Rather they suggest a fitting conclusion to the aftermath of the controversy and its confusion and divisions.

> Important discoveries in the way of curved-base pipes, copper axes, inscribed tablets, and other objects, mostly from the mounds of Scott and Louisa counties, made the Davenport Academy known nationally, even internationally, and aroused to activity a considerable part of the scientific talent of the state. The contributors to the early

volumes of the *Proceedings* of the Academy formed a notable group indeed: C. E. Putnam, R. J. Farquharson, John [*sic*] Gass, Wm. H. Holmes, Charles E. Harrison, W. H. Pratt, Frederick Starr; and it is impossible not to feel in their papers and discussions the inspiration under which they worked. (Keyes 1920:357).

If Keyes was later to change his mind about "inspiration," "inscribed tablets" and Harrison, Pratt, Putnam, and the Reverend Jacob Gass, he did not mention it in his publications over the next thirty years.

Matters rested until 1930. At the express invitation of the Davenport Museum—successor to the Academy—Dr. Henry Shetrone made a study of the specimens. His negative report was not unexpected. His other conclusions that over half of the collection of 65 platform pipes were fakes leads to a much more comprehensive understanding of the archaeology of the period. This implication is followed in Chapter 14, "The Conspiracy." It is enough to say here that Shetrone's reports (1930MS, 1930MSa) went unpublished and for this reason failed to resolve publicly the original controversy. Almost two decades later, John Bailey, who was then director of the museum, came upon additional evidence, but his summary (Bailey 1948) was published in such an obscure periodical that it failed to gain the circulation it deserved.

A Solution of the Davenport Mystery

13

Donald Herold became director of the Davenport Museum in 1959, inheriting a vast clutter of collections of specimens, books, and papers crammed inside the old museum building and in some downtown offices. The obsolete main building had been erected in 1878 by the Davenport Academy (plate 18), the museum's predecessor. It was joined by a passageway to an old, structurally unsound stone church taken over many years previously for storage and exhibits. Under Herold's administration, long deferred plans to build a new museum building were carried out; and, in the course of organizing the collections and files for the move, various manuscripts and letters were found. Herold also learned from a long-time staff member, Mrs. Ann Mizener, of Judge Bollinger's verbal account of the old controversy.

Previous museum directors had been interested in the controversy, and many of the most important papers were in a small cardboard box marked "Tiffany File." With the succession of directors broken up by time intervals, each incumbent had to learn the facts anew.

Bailey's Unsolved Mystery

In 1947 John H. Bailey, then director of the Davenport Musuem, gave a talk to his fellow members of the Contemporary Club of Davenport. This group, restricted by its bylaws to thirty-three regular members, existed as an organization from about 1895 until recently, printing a yearly report of the members' talks given to each other. During the club's existence, from about 1896-1967, seventy consecutive volumes were printed. Because of the small size of the membership, one could fairly say that Bailey's report belongs to that ephemeral class of manuscripts, printed but not published; to the best of my knowledge it has never been previously cited, nor is it available in some of the biggest libraries of the state. John H. Bailey died under tragic circumstances in 1948 before he had time to publish a fuller corrected report and include a bibliography.

Bailey, briefly, and somewhat informally, summarized the discovery and debates over the tablets and elephants. He entitled his paper "An

Unsolved Davenport Mystery" because the perpetrator of the forgeries was not known to him.

> As in all mystery stories, the search for "who-done-it" is the main objective and always the author has the answer in the last chapter. In this case, we shall have to be different—for the name of the culprit, if such he may be called, is still unknown; and therein lies the mystery. All the participants in this case, which focused the eyes of the scientific world upon Davenport, have long since passed away. At this late date, the clues are gone and all that remains are the objects in question themselves, and the various reports on them which are to be found in all the scientific libraries of the world. (Bailey 1948:3).

Bailey continued with his view that the maker of these objects

> either had a grudge against the Academy or he wished, because he was a friend of the Academy that it should be the first to show the world actual remains proving the contemporaneousness of the mound builder and the mastodon.

As for the role of the Reverend Jacob Gass, Bailey wrote,

> What better person to find his frauds and announce them to the world could the faker have chosen than a man of God whose integrity was unquestioned? Especially when that minister spent every free moment digging in the mounds. . . . In all sincerity Gass believed in his finds, and as I have pointed out—he was merely a means to an end. (Bailey 1948: 8-9).

After giving this talk, Bailey learned that his "unsolved mystery" had a solution, and that each of his previous surmises was wrong. The object of the hoax was neither to aid nor detract from the Academy but was aimed at making a fool of Gass himself. The clues were not gone, nor had all of the participants' knowledge passed away. Gass may have believed in his finds "in all sincerity" at first but eventually learned the truth. He was not "merely a means to an end" but, if we may twist a phrase, Gass was the end of the means. The story of how Bailey learned the solution, too late to include it in the posthumously published 1948 summary of the case, is contained in the Hurlbut transcript.

The Hurlbut Transcript

Irving Hurlbut was born in Muscatine, and his family subsequently moved to Davenport, where he grew up and lived for fifty years. He was an auditor at the Union Savings Bank of Davenport and upon retirement sixteen years ago moved back to Muscatine. He currently is a justice of the peace and runs a small tourist shop sellings rocks, minerals, and artifacts. While employed in Davenport, Mr. Hurlbut knew various directors and worked as a volunteer for the museum. Over a period of twenty years, he went on field trips with the directors, collecting information on Indian mounds and working at the excavations. When the museum was between directors, he helped in changing displays.

Having learned from the museum staff that Mr. Hurlbut knew the story of the frauds, I arranged a visit to his house in March 1969. J. N. Young had previously met him in connection with the geology of the area, and I had heard of him as a knowledgeable amateur archaeologist, but I was not yet personally acquainted with him. We made a written record of the discussion, reviewed it, and the typed copy was sent back to him for corrections and additions. The following statements and questions appear in more detail in the twelve-page typed transcript (Hurlbut 1969MS).

The Bollinger Account of the Davenport Frauds

Judge Bollinger lived on East Locust Street in Davenport and his hobby was the study of Abraham Lincoln. He was highly respected all over town. The late John Bailey, former Director of the Davenport Museum and I were always together. The Judge figured we knew the entire history of the archaeology of Scott County and so he said to us, "The doctor told me I have only six months to live and I wanted somebody to know about the Davenport tablets and pipes." He invited both of us to have lunch with him at his hideaway in the Chamber of Commerce Building located at the N.W. corner of 4th and Main Streets. He said to the waiter when he came to his private room, "Bring us three of the usual." Neither Bailey nor I were what you would call drinking men and we were just dumbfounded at their size. These were followed by a delicious dinner. It was then that he told us the story . . . I will try to put it in the Judge's words as I remember them.

The Judge told us: "We had no respect for Reverend Gass because he was the biggest windjammer and liar and everyone knew he was. We wanted to shut him up once and for all. So I went down to the Old Slate House and went to the back of the building where nobody could see what I was doing and tore off a number of the old slates. The entire building was covered with slates. I took the slates up to the Academy basement where the old gang met.

"Well this group would go to the Academy and have a bull session because there wasn't anyplace else to go. They used to have a few drinks and just shoot the breeze. The janitor was in with us. We had two old almanacs, one German and one Hebrew, and we copied out of them and inscribed the hieroglyphics on those slate tablets, and things we just made up—anything that would confuse them, especially Gass.

"That fall Gass was digging down at the Cook Mounds. Cold weather had just set in and we knew Gass wouldn't dig anymore 'til spring. So we carved the slate tablet and several of the pipes and to make the pipes look old we covered them with oil that was on the janitor's workbench. He had more time to work on these things than we did.

"Then some of the boys went up to Tiffany's house because we knew he had a collection of minerals. Tiffany wasn't home at the time but to be sure everyone knew it was a joke, his wife gave us one of his best quartz crystals, one that Gass had seen many times and admired. She thought it was a pretty good joke. The shell and red ocher we got from the museum.

"We went over to Schmidt's Quarry and carried the pieces of limestone and built a little pyramid over the tablet and crystal and shell. The shell was from the Gulf of Mexico. We knew in the spring of the year he'd start digging again.

"Sure enough he went down there again when the weather warmed and came back with the stuff and we just shut up and let him rave and rant.

"First thing we knew the unusual find was published in Europe as well as in this country and spread like wildfire. By then it was too late to say anything about it. Tiffany wouldn't even admit at the time that it was his crystal, but later on of course he admitted it.

"I just wanted somebody to know it was all a fake. It was all made in the basement. We were all in on it."

Judge Bollinger at the time said, "I still have those old slates in the basement of my house. Come up some time and get all of them. Get them all out of here. At the same time I'll show you my Lincoln collection. I've just completed arrangements with the State of Iowa to give it to the University and it will be the last time you will get a chance to see it.

I went up to his house to get the slate pieces and he said, "Take the whole bunch. Get them out of here."

There were a number of them in an old bushel basket, perhaps a dozen. I still have some of them. You can see nail holes in some of them, just like the nail holes in one of the tablets. (Hurlbut 1969MS).

Replies and Discussion

Mr. Hurlbut gave The University of Iowa Archaeological Laboratory the slate tablet he had in his living room (plate 19). It has a nail hole the same diameter as those of the Calendar stone (plate 3): three-eighths of an inch. The other tablets from Judge Bollinger were in storage and not accessible because of high water in the Mississippi. We asked a number of questions to clarify some problems.

Question: What was the old Slate House?

Reply: It was an old elaborate "sporting house" [house of prostitution] known up and down the Mississippi, and the steamboats tied right up in front of it. It had a slate roof and slates nailed on the outside walls. It was located at what is now the Davenport entrance of the Government Bridge. . . .

Question: This specimen you are showing me (plate 19) is a greenish slate and the tablets are black shale. Why is this? . . . Were all the slates on the building alike?

Reply: No, they were different thicknesses, different sizes, different colors, and were laid on the side of the building in geometrical patterns or designs like stars. I can confirm this because there is a published picture. Huebinger published a book of all the beautiful houses and businesses of Davenport many years ago. . . .

Question: [relative to the pencil-like designs on the Hunting Scene tablet (plate 2).]

Reply: . . . There is nothing on here that is anything like signs used in any Masonic ritual. They look a little like quartz crystals, like the one they got at Tiffany's house.

Question: The circles [on the Calendar tablet, plate 3] were evidently made with a steel compass.

Reply: Yes, because the center hole is there to prove it.

Question: Did Judge Bollinger ever comment on this?

Reply: No he did not.

Question: I would now like to show you plate 4, the limestone tablet.

Reply: This was never brought up, but at the time he said ". . . We got the limestone at Schmidt's Quarry," but he never said ". . . we got thin slabs" or that they carved on it.

Question: Pratt in his unpublished report to the Committee of Investigation in 1886 called it Smith's Quarry. [Pratt, 1886MS, denied that anything could have been planted in the mound because Smith's Quarry lay close by.] Are you sure that Schmidt is correct?

Reply: Yes. Schmidt's Quarry is located about 1,000 feet N.W. of the Mounds—at the time that was all a part of the Cook Farm. The quarry hole can still be seen on the road to Credit Island, on the left or east side of the road, just as you cross the railroad tracks. It is now filled with water. . . .

Question: From your account as you told it to me, it would seem Judge Bollinger is talking about both mounds which contained tablets? . . .

Reply: I would answer by saying that he constantly referred to them as all in a group. He didn't say Mound 1, Mound 2, Mound 3, or the like.

Question: Can you explain why Judge Bollinger did not become a member of the Academy until 1887?

Reply: I have no idea.

Question: Do you have any idea who the other principals were?

Reply: Do you mean the gang that used to meet up there for bull sessions? . . . Well, there was Pratt and Tiffany, Harrison. Putnam was never there—he was aloof. It was his money and he always thought he was a little better than the rest of them.

Question: Would you recognize any other names?

Reply: . . . I was not personally acquainted with any of them. . . .
(Barris) Uncertain.
(Farquharson) Yes that man was in it.
(Lindley) Yes, that name . . .
(George French) I knew a Decker French.
(Parry) Yes . . .
(J. Duncan Putnam) I heard of him but that was all.

Question: I now show you plate 5 [Elephant Pipes]. Do you recall any of Judge Bollinger's remarks about these specimens? . . .

Reply: Judge Bollinger said that there was one of the pipes that a farmer had smoked for years, and one of the Academy members dropped and broke it, so they bought it anyhow. The Judge said this and the partridge [from Toolesboro] were genuine. [plate 5.2; plate 12.1].

Question: What about the other elephant [plate 5.1]?

Reply: All I can remember [the Judge saying was] there was a fit made over the first elephant, how there never was an elephant found around there; and they went and made another elephant and a lot of other things. They made them out of softer material that they could carve easily.

Question: Do you recall, were these pipes drilled or just carved?

Reply: All he said was, "we carved them." To make them look old they rubbed them with oil and put oil in the bowl—just let them sit and soak—oil that was on the janitor's long workbench in the basement of the old Academy.

Question: I am showing you pictures of the other pipes [plates 6-10 labeled Pipe Frauds].

Reply: I don't know anything about those. Some of the so-called fakes look good in the pictures. . . .

Question: Do you have any specific information that Pratt [the curator] knew there were platform pipes being made in the basement?

Reply: I would assume from what Judge Bollinger said—that "we were all in on it, we went down and started making pipes in the basement, and the other stuff"—that he knew. . . .

Question: Do you know anything else about Reverend Blumer? [The brother-in-law of Gass found the second elephant pipe in the excavation.]

Reply: Only that everyone said he was the same kind of fellow as Gass was. Nobody believed anything he said. . . .

Question: Did you ever hear any specific stories about Reverend Gass?

Reply: [Nothing] except that he went off and bought some pottery and brought it back to the museum, and tried to tell people he had dug it up himself. But the other people knew he had bought it and it was not local.

Question: Where did he buy it?

Reply: Some of it was Arkansas and some of it was Florida pottery —it certainly wasn't local. I don't know where he bought it all.

Question: Have you ever seen any of this pottery in the museum?

Reply: Yes, all of it, years ago. I don't know if it's there yet.

Question: If we showed you the pottery from Cook's Farm, would you know which was local and which was bought?

Reply: Yes, I think so.

Question: Can you tell me where the Cook Farm Mounds were located?

Reply: The Cook Mound site was known as Cook's Farm or Cook's Point. The Thompson-Hayward Chemical Company is now built right on top of the mound location (2040 W. River St.). This would have been a beautiful location for a mound site because there was a creek running down on the west side of the site all the way to the Mississippi River. The river was about 1,000 feet east of the mounds. (Hurlbut 1969MS).

The Conspiracy

14

Judge Bollinger marred the case by exaggerations and failing to write down a factual summary. Many parts of the story are confirmed by documents and manuscripts. Other parts of the narrative provide unsubstantiated but plausible explanations more difficult to verify. Within the latter group are the sources of the slate and limestone, the manufacture of the second elephant in the basement, the role and behavior of the Reverend Jacob Gass, and the extent to which Academy members were involved in the frauds. Unfortunately there are chronological problems.

The narrative, in the form it has been preserved, is obviously based on information and stories obtained in later years. I believe the judge embellished the tale, and for this reason it is necessary to place his role and probable sources of information within a biographical perspective.

James Wills Bollinger

Some information on Judge Bollinger is available in Special Collections at The University of Iowa Library. He was born in 1867 in Geneseo, Illinois, a town east of Davenport, and his family moved to Davenport when he was six years old. It can thus be confirmed that James Bollinger was only nine years old in the fall of 1876 when the slate tablets were put into the Cook mound and had not yet reached the age of ten when Gass unearthed them again in 1877. Furthermore, the cornerstone of the Academy building was laid in 1877, after the slate tablets were found. The building was not dedicated and occupied until 1878—more than a month after the limestone tablet was excavated from another Cook mound. Although the Davenport conspiracy had childish aspects in the beginning, we need not waste time speculating whether a boy of nine led it in a nonexistent basement. Whatever the judge may have said, he was nowhere near the scene of the events he so vividly described.

It is possible the tablets were made by members in the Odd Fellows Hall. Before their building was completed, the Academy rented back rooms from the Odd Fellows for storage of specimens and meetings.

Many of the fraudulent pipes were made in the Academy's new building, and this is the gist of some of Lindley's remarks. These pipes first appeared in 1879 and thereafter with regularity until late 1882 when Gass left town. A number of donations of conspicuous frauds, collected and purchased in 1882, were given to the Academy with great ceremony early in 1883 and were reported in *Science* and elsewhere. They were no longer being made in 1883. The principal donor was Gass' brother Edwin Gass. He was not a member, and nothing is known of him except that he moved to Postville with his brother and, I believe, ran a saloon. Edwin later returned to Switzerland. This brother remains a shadowy figure but seems to have helped in the purchase and collection of specimens.

In 1885, Bollinger graduated from Davenport High School and did not join the Academy until 1887, a decade after the tablets were found. He was attending The University of Iowa in Iowa City at the time he joined, and there is no reference to him in the *Proceedings* beyond his membership. Bollinger was not active in Academy affairs at this period of his life and was not resident in the town.

After practicing law in Davenport, he served on the bench of the Seventh Judicial District of the state from 1897 to 1911, when he resigned to go into business, retaining the courtesy title of judge. Prominent and successful, he was president of the State Bar Association in 1909 and later of two Davenport companies. Among numerous clubs and associations, Bollinger maintained his membership in the Academy; and after it had developed into the Davenport Museum, he was elected president of the museum board. With a wide circle of friends, including a number of men with first- or second-hand knowledge of the affair, the judge undoubtedly came to know the main outlines of the story he retold in the first person.

Judge Bollinger was widely appreciated as a gourmet and raconteur. His favorite recipes were published in a national magazine which has some anecdotes about this side of his life. In addition to these activities, he had amassed a major collection of Lincoln books and memorabilia given to the University. A check of this collection shows he left no private papers that might elucidate the Davenport controversy. The storyteller, we can imagine, presented a most dramatic account to his two listeners. The judge died in 1951, three years after John Bailey, whom he had chosen to help preserve his secret history of the frauds.

In the course of sending the transcript back to Mr. Hurlbut for corrections, I wrote him about the chronological problems. He replied by letter insisting that the narrative was essentially correct in the form it stood, and to the best of his memory, it was the way it had been told to Bailey and himself some twenty years ago. He added that John Bailey and he had discussed it many times. Bailey was of the opinion that retelling the story would just cause trouble and they had better keep quiet about it. In the 1950s there were four different museum directors. He mentioned the matter to each of them, and the first three said he should keep quiet about it. "It might give the museum a bad name . . . and no one would believe it now because there were no living witnesses to the occasion." He received a more interested and knowledgeable reception from Donald Herold. The letter from Irving Hurlbut (1969MSa) concludes, "But that is my story, and it is the truth, and I am going to stick to it, and I don't care if anyone believes me or not."

The Hurlbut transcript and slate tablet (plate 19) have the ring of authenticity, but one must accept the limitations of a secondary account originating from a nonparticipant. It is as close as we shall be able to come to the solution of some parts of the Davenport mystery.

Jacob Gass, Victim of All

We have no reason to question the integrity of Jacob Gass in *originally* believing that all his finds were authentic. His later work was dedicated to the Academy's interests, and the early catalogued collections in archaeology are largely due to his efforts. He gave his finds to the Academy.

His enthusiasm quickened after finding the tablets. Duncan Putnam, secretary of the Academy, wrote in 1880 that although mounds are very numerous "not one in ten contains anything of value." This, he added, does not discourage Mr. Gass. "After opening, say, twenty or more mounds without result, he will commence the next with as much vigor as the first." (cited by C. E. Putnam 1886:264). The statement about the number of mounds is no exaggeration. In a brief published note, Gass (1882a:140-146) reported with disappointment the few artifacts obtained in 1879-1880 although 75 mounds were explored in little more than a year's time under his direction with Academy funds. It was not, despite the excavation total, more than a somewhat part-time occupation with him. The extent of mound pillaging, for such rapid digging can be dignified by no better term, is astonishing. That no one at the Academy questioned such destruction is symptomatic of the period. Artifacts, not information, was the goal of the mound explorers and the institutions that supported them.

After moving to Postville, Gass came to recognize the bitter truth. In preparing his defense statement for *Science,* he wrote Pratt about Stevens' correspondence, saying:

> Oh, it has been such a dreadful carelessness in me to let such letters be written and sent away without examining the contents, and I must now suffer severely enough for this carelessness. Oh when will this storm be past and peace restored, for which I long so much!— Of late I have often thought how happy are the dead, whose rest cannot be disturbed, compared with such an unfortunate being as I am, who has been the victim of all. (Gass 1886MS).

It appears that by 1886, if not earlier, "the victim of all" realized frauds had been perpetrated on him. If this was his meaning, it was rigorously suppressed by Pratt and Putnam. His defense published in *Science* passed through their hands. In reading it, and indeed every note Gass published, one finds he never made any claim for the genuineness of the specimens.

A Visit to Postville

In 1969, the author learned from J. N. Young that descendants of Gass still lived in Postville. An interview followed with a daughter, Hertha Gass Erbe, and a son, Arthur Gass. This confirmed that Gass did know he had been hoaxed by his Academy associates.

Mr. Arthur Gass, now 84 years old, said his father had talked about the affair, knew he had been tricked, and did mention the name of "someone who was jealous of him" who had been part of the hoax. Mr. Arthur Gass could not remember this name, nor could he recognize it as any of the Academy people mentioned to him.

> Question: Did he say anything about the elephant pipe? (showing a picture of it owned by the Gass family)
> Reply: . . . Just that they had made things and buried them and he dug them up.
> Question: Do you recall that he said anything about this? (A picture of the slate tablet. The picture was owned by the Gass family.)
> Reply: No. . . . just that they dug down by the river in the mounds down by Muscatine. . . .

> Question: Did he ever talk about the pipes or tablets? Was any-
> thing said about them being planted?
> Reply: Not the tablets, he never mentioned those; just spearheads,
> arrowheads, stuff like that.

Also interviewed, Mrs. Erbe said that her father had talked about the events at Davenport, but not a great deal, and that he knew he had been "fooled." The above remarks, from the transcript written at the time of the interview, are on file with the other documents (Gass Erbe 1969MS).

Gass Litigation

A resident of Postville and local historian, Mr. Stan Schroeder, has copies of the local Postville newspaper from the 1890s not available in either Iowa City or Des Moines. He has sent a typewritten copy of excerpts (Schroeder 1969MS) which provide an interesting sidelight on the central figure of the controversy.

Jacob Gass left Davenport at the age of forty, in 1882, to take the pulpit of St. John's Lutheran Church in Postville. He had an active and successful ministry for a decade and organized the construction of a large new church in 1890. In 1892, Gass resigned the pastorate, but his congregation refused to accept the resignation. The same year, he founded the *Iowa Volksblatt,* a German newspaper to rival the two English papers in town. His venture was apparently an expense, and in 1893 Gass joined a leasing speculation which failed. He and an associate were successfully sued for $300, and Gass in turn began a libel suit against the editor of the rival newspaper over the published reports and other remarks that had appeared about the matter. By the end of the year, his congregation voted to release him from the pastorate, and the Lutheran Church at Cresco, Iowa, unanimously invited him. He declined, left the ministry in 1894, sold his interest in the *Volksblatt,* and bought a farm at the south edge of town.

In 1896, a furor arose over a promissory note for $500 dated 1894. Gass testified that an insurance man, Mr. A. P. Hale, had forged Gass' name on it. Hale was indicted, arrested in Dubuque, and brought to Waukon. Hale, *protesting his innocence, spent five months in jail,* awaiting trial.

> When his case was called, the complaining witness Gass was con-
> spicuous by his absence. He recently returned to Postville and

> Hale having received information that he was about to take his departure for Germany for an indefinite sojourn, swore out papers for his arrest. . . . The big Rev. Gass trial is on at the county seat at Waukon this week, and lawyers and ever so many of our citizens are in attendance as advisors and witnesses. (Schroeder 1969MS:7-8).

Gass, charged with perjury, was released on bond. The grand jury, meeting in 1896, did not indict him. A rehearing was, however, scheduled over the previous civil suit.

At the earlier suit, Hale, found guilty of forgery, was made responsible for the payment of the $500 note. In 1897, the case came to trial again. The lawyers defending Gass had a difficult time.

> They had to fight the most prominent attorneys in the county . . . and what was equally bad, the united prejudice of the Waukon people and very largely the people of the entire county. (Ibid., 8).

The jury deliberated a day and a night. At 4 A.M. the next morning, they reached the decision that Gass was innocent.

The loser, Hale, became involved in other difficulties almost immediately. He was charged with embezzling $100 from his insurance company in Dubuque and ran up unpaid bills during his dramatic escape. Reaching Omaha, he committed suicide in 1897. "Thus ends," the newspaper reported, "the career of a somewhat notorious character in these parts." (Ibid., 9).

Gass prospered in farming and retired in 1910, building a large home near the Lutheran Church at the edge of his farm. He died in 1925. The Davenport conspiracy had so discouraged him that he gave up archaeology and took up geology as a hobby.

Gass was a very capable and deeply religious man with a number of intellectual interests. As the central figure in the Davenport affair, his later career is a matter of public record and great relevance. In his perjury and forgery trials of 1896 and 1897, he was tried by jury and was found innocent.

The Conspirators

The only man confessing to participation in the frauds is Bollinger who was too young to be involved. The slate tablets in his possession document the origin of the artifacts, but we suspect he obtained them from one of the actual participants at a much later date. As a lifelong member of the Academy, he came to know the men involved and heard the stories circulating around the Davenport area. By implicating himself and mentioning no names beyond saying "we were all in on it," he insured that any promise of secrecy would be kept when the story passed beyond the museum into the public domain. His opening narrative contains no names. Those mentioned in the questions were part of a well-known group meeting informally, and individually they may not have been responsible.

The Academy was a clubhouse during a period when there were few respectable activities in town to occupy an educated man's time. Some but not all of the membership became involved in various ways in the frauds. An example can be seen in the unfolding of the elephant pipe riddle. Someone must have planted the first one with the farmer in Louisa County. Whoever was responsible may have been a member, because news reached Tiffany and he unsuccessfully attempted to warn Gass about it. His warning was ignored (Pratt 1886MS). Other regulars, not informed of the elephant's antecedents, watched the creation of a more realistic second edition, having no better reason than "there was a fit made over the first." (Hurlbut 1969MS). The discoverer of it, the brother-in-law of Gass himself, was implicated by Lindley's rhetorical question, "Did the Rev. Mr. Blumer ever have a, knowingly, fraudulent curved-base elephant pipe in his possession?" (Preston 1885-1886MS). The janitor's homemade elephant pipe was carried out of the Academy by Blumer (Phelps 1886MS). Various fabricated pipe specimens appearing in the excavations from 1880-1882 show a curious cycle. The janitor, Graham, sometimes accompanied by a later member, Toellner, visited sites months before some of the pipe frauds were excavated. His tools, his oil, his workbench, and indeed, he himself are specified. Lindley mentioned the tools (Preston 1886 MS); Bollinger tells of the rest. Graham admitted making pipes but denied they appeared in the excavations (Phelps 1886MS). The janitor was but one of the craftsmen, and the regular members hanging out at the Academy club manufactured other pipes. Lindley claimed Tiffany made relics in the basement (McCowen 1886MSa).

Another example of the complications is the charge that C. E. Harrison made arrowheads. Lindley stated his charge in committee and at the general meeting (Preston 1885-1886MS, McCowen 1886MS), referring to a boast of making a 3,000-year-old arrowhead in five minutes. Pratt claimed Lindley also chipped flint (Phelps 1886MS). Gass told his children that arrowheads had been planted in his excavations (Gass Erbe 1969MS). Can we connect these accounts?

This same Harrison "is a stone cutter" (Tiffany 1882MS), a former occupation not disputed (Tiffany 1886MS), and Lindley asks "Have stone and marble cutters ever made tablets of hieroglyphics and passed them off for genuine relics of antiquity?" (Preston 1885-1886MS). Despite the suspicions of Tiffany and Lindley, I believe Harrison accepted the limestone tablet as genuine in good faith and was not told about that prank. If he did not have a hand in its manufacture, he probably made others—perhaps the five found by Gass in Cleona Township, a donation subsequently missing from the collections. If my surmises are correct, Harrison knew only part of the story concerning the fabrication of specimens.

The excavations during Iowa winters have a ludicrous scientific aspect. The slates planted in fall of 1876 were dug out in January. The limestone tablet placed in an adjacent mound the next year again required a January excavation to recover it. Frozen ground concealed the disturbance. That this concealment was felt necessary strengthens the innocence of Gass and Harrison in making these finds. Both had knowledge of other falsifications, Harrison as mentioned previously. Gass had some dealings with conspicuous frauds sent to Stevens as trades (Berlin 1886, 1886a, Thomas in Berlin 1886MS). We are unable to evaluate or confirm the story of Gass purchasing Florida and Arkansas pottery, passing it off as local (Hurlbut 1969MS). He came to know some frauds were being made, such as arrowheads, but seems to have continued to believe in the tablets, for he did not mention them to his children as fabrications. Like everyone else involved, Gass and Harrison had partial knowledge and suppressed it.

In the same way, incomplete information characterizes Tiffany's grasp of the affair. He was suspicious of the elephants and limestone tablet and wrote the Bureau of Ethnology about it (Tiffany 1882MS). Despite this information, he accepted the slate tablets as genuine. His letter of 1882 came four years after the limestone tablet and he did not mention the crystal story which he told locally (Bailey 1948, Pratt 1886MS), although his wife could confirm the story. He was one of the few who had second thoughts about joining the conspiracy to suppress information. They were, however, second thoughts, for at first he denied all knowledge of the crystal taken from his collection (Hurlbut 1969MS).

Pratt's Business College was across the street from the Academy, and he was constantly in and out of the building during the day to such an extent they appointed him curator. It is almost inconceivable that he did not know pipes were being made in the evening sessions, since they must have been visible in the basement, aging with the oil treatment. The janitor claimed Pratt saw the elephant. He, Gass, and Farquharson were sufficiently curious about one of the pipes which "smelled like putty" that they tested it (unsuccessfully) with hot iron to determine the oil content (Pratt 1886MS). No one told Pratt that the tablets were frauds, although he apparently knew about the second elephant pipe, if it is the one made by Graham. He failed to connect the various activities together, to give him the benefit of the doubt.

There were others involved who had partial knowledge, for Lindley made the claim, "Some of the most respected members of this Academy believe these tablets to be a fraud." (McCowen 1886MS). Even Farquharson, embarrassed, but accepting the tablets (1877), backed down almost immediately and suggested the Mormons planted them (1877a).

Perhaps the closest approximation to explaining the whole deplorable scandal can be reached by saying certain regulars made frauds, and others possessed information about these activities carried out under the aegis of the Academy. Putnam and his wife ran the business side of the organization, paying an increasing share of the bills as time went on, but did not belong to the inner circle of regulars who spent their time at the Academy clubhouse. No one dared tell them, and indeed, no one seems to have known enough to link all the falsifications together.

The Conspiracy

There is a tendency on the part of some to dismiss fabrications as jokes, or pay no further attention to them once they are exposed. I have taken this affair seriously, spending a great deal of time on it. The controversy should not be lightly dismissed as a series of pranks, for it is a very rare phenomenon, an archaeological conspiracy, which sheds light on the weakness of organized research in the nineteenth century.

Men met in secret and planned falsifications. When the artifacts took on scientific importance as supporting evidence in the mound builder controversies, the men agreed among themselves to suppress the truth. Others made effigy pipes. Men outside the Academy began selling frauds to the Academy itself. Other fraudulent artifacts were traded across the country, and even some plaster geological specimens began to appear in the collections. The conspiracy took a more vicious turn in the expulsion and social humiliation of members who tried to explain. Threats of libel were used in an attempt at intimidation. Distortions of fact, errors, and ridicule began to occur in leading scientific journals. The controversy boiled on in some quarters until the turn of the century, leading a few archaeologists astray into the 1920s.

I have not attempted to damn the men involved. The documentary evidence bears its own responsibility, and there are certain to be distortions when attempting to search out the secrets of nearly a century ago. The purpose has been to show a rather wide involvement among members of a scientific association in the manufacture of frauds. If few men actually made them, knowledge that they were being made was fairly common. It is also apparent the sordid means by which secrecy was maintained and the truth suppressed. The Davenport conspiracy is an almost unbelievable degradation of scientific research.

The Decline of the Academies

The Davenport conspiracy is more tangled and complicated than the well-known Kensington and Piltdown examples of fraud (See Wahlgren 1958 and Weiner 1955). The genuine Hopewell artifacts obtained by Gass and his contemporaries are extremely interesting, and the work they undertook and published began systematic explorations in the state. It is tragic that controversy and fraud overshadowed this contribution.

On a broader view, the numerous Davenport frauds typify some of the scientific difficulties in the nineteenth century when full-time research was rare. Amateurs, well meaning but undisciplined in the traditions of scientific investigation and ethics, frequently caused the greatest confusions. The survival of the specimens and documentation provides one of the most detailed case studies of this period in American archaeology, and, I think, of the history of science in this country.

The difficult transition from amateur to professional research was underway. In larger cities and towns throughout the country, volunteer scientific societies and associations were common. The breakdown of the Davenport Academy was symbolic of the weakness inherent in most of these academies. Over the subsequent decades, those groups which survived did so by largely giving up the function of research, becoming museums dedicated to exhibits and education. It was an important new role. It was also very different from the nineteenth century enthusiasms and excesses flourishing under the assumption that scientific research was easy and intellectual qualifications were unimportant.

By the turn of the century, most of the local city academies had become conspicuously obsolete; few new ones formed, many died quietly, and those which persisted were social clubs. It was obvious what had happened. Regional universities built around independent academic departments had created a new system for organized research. The Davenport conspiracy illustrates the disorders which could occur in the small private organizations which flourished earlier in the United States.

Appendix
The Evidence of the Frauds

The elephant pipes and tablets lay at the center of the controversy, but a study of the entire collection is relevant because slightly more than half of the collection of Davenport platform pipes were forgeries.

The Tablets

> Everybody who knew anything about ancient relics knew these tablets to be recent. Any stone-cutter would say so. Anybody who knew anything about glue and cement would say so. The man who helped find them said the account of their finding was not true. The man who owned the farm upon which the mound was located said it was not true. Everybody knew that bogus relics were manufactured from time to time in various places. These relics were, as everybody agreed, manufactured. We had a man in the area who boasted he could make such things. Anybody could draw the conclusions. (Lindley as recorded by McCowen 1886MSb).

Plate 1. Cremation Scene tablet, size 12 by 9½ inches, broken during excavation and repaired. It is carved from black shale, obtainable locally. The inscription was inspired by two old almanacs or Webster's Dictionary. Davenport Museum specimen AR 15338, fraud.

Plate 2. Hunting Scene tablet, reverse of cremation scene, but separated from it along the natural cleavage plane and unbroken. Size 10¼ by 12 inches. Davenport Museum specimen AR 15339, fraud.

Plate 3. Calendar Stone tablet, size 6¾ by 6¾ inches with two suspension holes ⅜ inch in diameter. The diameters of the rings inscribed with a steel compass are 2, 3½, 5, and 6¼ inches, the distances between them measuring about ¾ inch. The zodiac was copied from two old almanacs or Webster's Dictionary. No thickness measurements are given for the three shale tablets since they are imbedded in plaster of Paris bordered by wooden frames. Davenport Museum specimen AR 15341, fraud.

Plate 19. Judge Bollinger's slate tablet, said to be a shingle from the Old Slate House, a house of prostitution, where the stone was presumably obtained to make the tablets. Maximum dimensions are 8 by 5½ and 15/16 inches thick. Only one sawed edge is present, the other three sides being broken and incomplete. The material is green slate, imported from the East and not available locally. The inscribed tablets of black shale could be a local material. The Slate House had different colors of shale and slate shingles. Two drilled holes are present for nailing the shingle to a wall or roof. The dimensions of the holes are different, one being ½ and the other ⅜ inches—but the correspondence to the calendar stone holes (⅜ inches) is sufficient to identify the shale inscribed tablets as shingles although the exact source may be questioned. University of Iowa Archaeological Laboratoty specimen 199-1, contributed by Irving Hurlbut.

Plate 4.·Limestone tablet with Indian figure, size 12 by 7 inches; 1½ inches thick. Broken when found and subsequently repaired. The Indian axe and pipe representations were brightly painted with red ocher. Note that the eyes of the platform pipe designs have quartz inset eyes, glued with white cement. The illustration is taken from the Davenport *Proceedings* (PDANS 2: pl VII) since the quartz eyes are now missing. The limestone is said to have come from Schmidt's Quarry nearby. Mr. C. E. Harrison, later president of the Academy and discoverer of the tablet, vigorously denied he made it. Davenport Museum specimen AR 15342, fraud.

The Concretion

Dr. Lindley's foregoing remarks about cement and glue become clearer when one compares the concretion with glued quartz eyes and those affixed to the limestone inscribed tablet. The concretion was found on the surface after Jacob Gass completed his excavation for the slate tablets. As Thomas (1885) pointed out, this seemed to link the limestone and slate tablets together, although they were found in two mounds.

Plate 16. (lower). Limestone concretion with glued quartz eyes. Scale is in inches. The two views are taken from the *Proceedings* (PDANS 2:256-257) since the quartz eyes are now missing from the specimen. The specimen (AR 15092) was found in the backdirt of·Mound 3, Cook Farm.

Excavations at Cook Farm

The tablets were found in two mounds at Cook Farm which had previously been disturbed. This fact led professional archaeologists, among them Foreman, Thomas, and Peet, to the conclusion that the tablets were intrusive, or "planted".

Plate 15. Mound 3 at Cook Farm, cross section and vertical views. Grave A is the burial pit excavated by Gass in 1874 with undisturbed primary burials. Grave B is the burial pit he excavated in 1877, finding the slate tablets among scattered and incomplete human bones. Foreman termed burial pit B "thoroughly ransacked." Other symbols as follows: (*a*) limestones one foot below surface; (*b*) human bones; (*c-c'*) upper shell layer; (*d-d'*) lower shell layer; (*e*) cavity excavated on the north side of grave A; (*f*) position of the tablets; (*s-s'*) shell layer bordered by a row or layer of rocks. Scale in feet. (PDANS 2:92-93).

Plate 16. Mound 11 at Cook Farm, cross section plan. The cavity in the rock cairn where the limestone tablet was found was used as evidence that the tablet had not been buried long. Symbols as follows: (*H*) undisturbed earth; (*T-T'*) original surface; (*X*) limestone rocks; (*A*) cavity in which the limestone tablet was found. Scale approximate and in feet. Drawing from PDANS 3:222. Judge Bollinger reported that the rock to build the cairn came from the nearby Schmidt Quarry.

The Academy and its Members

Some of the most central figures in the case were not photographed, or their pictures can not be identified in the museum records. The following men are illustrated from obituaries in the *Proceedings*.

R. J. Farquharson (1824-1884), president during 1878 when the first elephant and the limestone tablet were found (plate 17, upper left).

C. E. Putnam (1825-1887), prosecuting attorney for the defense of the tablets, and president who planned the expulsion of dissident members (plate 17, upper right).

W. H. Pratt (1822-1893), founder of the Academy, president in 1880 when the second elephant pipe was found, and later full-time curator (plate 17, lower left). He served as Putnam's right-hand man in fighting those within the Academy who questioned the specimens.

W. H. Barris (1821-1901), minister, teacher, and amateur geologist as well as a former president (plate 17, lower right). Barris, with Pratt, fought Tiffany over geological interpretations, and published a vitriolic attack against Tiffany. Barris served on the committee investigating Lindley and found none of the latter's charges could be sustained.

The Reverend Jacob Gass (1854-1925), discoverer or present when all the tablets and elephants were found and leader of the Academy's archaeological program (plate 20). The Davenport Museum has no picture of him. The photograph was copied from a family portrait, courtesy of Mrs. Hertha Gass Erbe.

Judge James Wills Bollinger (1867-1951), narrator of Old Slate House story; prominent Davenport attorney, businessman and president of the Davenport Museum Board, successor to the Academy (plate 19). He is shown with his Lincoln collection, later given to The University of Iowa. Photograph courtesy of The University of Iowa Library, Special Collections.

Mr. A. S. Tiffany, central figure in the arguments at the Academy, was expelled from membership after he wrote the Bureau of Ethnology in Washington that he believed the elephant pipes and the limestone tablet were frauds (plate 21). Unpublished photograph courtesy of the Davenport Public Museum.

The Davenport Academy in the 1880s, a social and scientific society, rephotographed from Starr (1897a:84). The basement workshop was used by Graham, Tiffany, Lindley, and others when making artifacts. Dr. Lindley practiced medicine in the building from about 1878 to 1884 (plate 18).

The Appraisal by Shetrone

In 1930, Dr. Henry C. Shetrone, director of the Ohio State Museum, and at that time probably the most knowledgeable American archaeologist on Hopewell culture, examined the specimens. He came by invitation extended by the director of the Davenport Museum, E. K. Putnam, who incidentally was a son of the redoubtable C. E. Putnam. Although the tablets were no longer at issue, there remained a belief that the elephant pipes might be genuine, but in any event, the director wished an honest professional opinion.

Shetrone's report (1930 MS) concluded that the tablets and elephants were frauds. In addition, Shetrone studied all the platform pipes in the Davenport collection and concluded in a detailed memorandum that only 31 of the 65 conformed to his criteria indicative of genuineness. Of the remainder, one was doubtful and 33 were fraudulent (1930 MSa). This was an astonishing and revealing conclusion. The author has restudied the 45 pipes still in the collection and in general concurs with Shetrone's identifications. The elephant pipes had been soaked in grease to give them an appearance of age, and Shetrone further noted shoe polish or equivalent material on another pipe. The remainder of the fabrications did not conform to specifications in material, shape, techniques, and proportions characteristic of Hopewellian specimens. By this time, 1930, the Academy *Proceedings* had become dormant, and the interesting Shetrone manuscripts remained unpublished in the files.

The Pipe Collection

In table 1 the missing pipes are listed by old catalogue numbers and information is summarized from various sources. The identification of genuineness or fabrication is taken from Shetrone's manuscript. The principal value of the table lies in the association of finders with finds, information which is discussed with the remainder of the pipe collection in a subsequent section.

Plates 5-10 are all of the fraudulent pipes currently in the Davenport Museum. Information on catalogue numbers, references, and finders are summarized in table 2. Shetrone's identification of each specimen as a fraud is accepted with but one exception. He listed the bear (plate 9.5) as indeterminate and withheld judgment. This study suggests it has the same characteristics as the other frauds: the bowl cavity is not at right angles to the platform, its material is limestone, the platform is rounded (the front part is missing), and the curved base is not pronounced. The length-width index of 4.3, however, is well within the genuine group.

Pipes Made by John Graham at the Academy. Three sketches (plate 18) were appended to the testimony he gave during Dr. Lindley's questions (Phelps 1886MS). He claimed he made these specimens and others including an elephant pipe at home. Under pressure, he admitted obtaining stone and doing some of the work in the Academy basement.

Plates 11-14 are "genuine" Hopewell specimens, so identified by Shetrone. After some doubts, we have come to be in general agreement with him. The pipe blank (plate 13.7) was misidentified as to material in the original publication and by Shetrone, both of whom termed it limestone. Microscopic evaluation by J. N. Young suggested it is welded tuff, from the West, possibly from Yellowstone. The form is appropriate, but it is the only example of this material in the collection. Information on these specimens is summarized in table 3.

Table 1

Platform Pipes Formerly in the Davenport Museum

Old Number	Shetrone[a] Evaluation	Bowl Shape	Provenience	Date	Collector	PDANS Reference
2923	Genuine	Plain	Iowa	1917	Paarman	—
2924	Genuine	Birdhead	SE Iowa	1914	Michelson	—
4446	Genuine	Plain	Cook farm	1874	Gass	1:117–143
4533	Genuine	Plain	Ill.	1875	French, Tiffany	1:114
4564	Genuine	Plain	SE Iowa	1877	Gass	2:150
4566	Genuine	Plain	Ill.	1877	Hall	3:48
4570	Genuine	Plain	—	—	Hall	—
7060	Genuine	Plain	SE Iowa	1880	Gass[b]	3:143
7389	Genuine	Plain	SE Iowa	1880	Gass[b]	3:145
7390	Genuine	Plain	SE Iowa	1880	Gass[b]	3:143, 145
7391	Genuine	Plain	SE Iowa	1880	Gass[b]	3:143, 145
8287	Genuine	Plain	Wis.	1883	Hall	4:233
7061	Fraud	Swan	SE Iowa	1880	Gronen[b]	3:145
7067	Fraud	Plain	Ill.	1880	Gass	3:138 (?)
7388	Fraud	Plain	Ill.	1880	Gass[b]	3:139
7619	Fraud	Serpent	Ill.	1880	Hitt	3:148
8275	Fraud	Plain	Ill.	1883	Ed. Gass[b]	4:222, 233
8280	Fraud	Eagle	Ill.	1883	Ed. Gass[b]	4:222, 233
8281	Fraud	Deer head	Ill.	1883	Ed. Gass[b]	4:222, 233
8284	Fraud	Animal	Ill.	1883	Ed. Gass[b]	4:222, 233
8357	Fraud	Plain	NE Iowa	1880	—	—

[a]Shetrone (1930MSa) evaluation of specimens subsequently missing from the collections.
[b]Donor or purchaser not identified as excavator.

Table 2
Identification of Fraudulent Pipes in the Davenport Museum

Plate	Bowl	Old Number	New Number	Date	Area	Collector	PDANS Reference
5.1	Elephant	6782	AR 14778	1880	SE Iowa	Blumer, Cass	3:133
5.2	Elephant	6355	AR 14779	1878	SE Iowa	Cass	2:348–239
5.3	Bear	8282	AR 14377	1883	Ill.	Ed. Gass[a]	4:222, 233
6.1	Bird	8286	AR 14383	1883	SE Iowa	Ed. Gass[a]	4:233
6.2	Bird	6783	AR 14497	1880	SE Iowa	Blumer, Cass	3:130, 133
6.3	Animal	4798	AR 14504	1882	SE Iowa	Cass, Ed. Gass	4:216 (?)
7.1	Human head	6786	AR 14491	1880	Mo.	Gass[a]	3:108
7.2	Beaver(?)	7798	AR 14373	1882	SE Iowa	Gass[a]	4:216
7.3	Beaver(?)	6785	AR 14374	1879	Ill.	Gass	3:137
8.1	Wolf	7387	AR 14381	1880	Ill.	Gass[a]	3:139
8.2	Lizard	7546	AR 14376	1880	Ill.	Gass[a]	3:147
8.3	Turtle	7624	AR 14375	—	Ill.	—	—
9.1	Beetle	7547	AR 14486	1880	Ill.	Gass[a]	3:147
9.2	Fox	8283	AR 14385	1883	Ill.	Ed. Gass[a]	4:222, 233
9.3	Bird	8278	AR 14372	1883	Ill.	Ed. Gass[a]	4:222, 233
9.4	Bird	8279	AR 14378	1883	Ill.	Ed. Gass[a]	4:222, 233
9.5	Bear	6732	AR 14370	—	SE Iowa	Gass	2:348
10.1	Plain	8273	AR 14499	1883	SE Iowa	Ed. Gass[a]	4:222, 233
10.2	Plain	8274	AR 14506	1883	SE Iowa	Ed. Gass[a]	4:222, 233
10.3	Plain	7622	AR 14509	1881	Ill.	Gass	3:186–192
10.4	Animal	7625	AR 14508	—	Ill.	—	—
10.5	Plain	8276	AR 14498	1883(?)	Ill.	Ed. Gass[a]	4:222, 233
10.6	Plain	7621	AR 14500	1881	Ill.	Gass	3:186–192
10.7	Plain	8285	AR 14505	1883	SE Iowa	Ed. Gass[a]	4:222, 233
10.8	Animal	8277	AR 14507	1882(?)	SE Iowa	Ed. Gass[a]	4:216 (?)

[a]Donor or purchaser not identified as excavator.

Table 3
Identification of Genuine Pipes in the Davenport Museum

Plate	Bowl	Old Number	New Number	Date	Area	Collector	PDANS Reference
11.1	Frog	4445	AR 15063	1874	Cook farm	Gass	1:117–143
11.2	Dog(?)	4490	AR 15065	1874	Cook farm	Gass	1:120
11.3	Bird	4450	AR 15105	1874	Cook farm	Schmidt	1:120
12.1	Bird	4562	AR 15025	1875	SE Iowa	Harrison	1:106–111
12.3	Bird	4563	AR 15026	1875	SE Iowa	Pratt, Harrison	1:106–111
12.5	Wildcat[a]	4558	AR 15030	1875	SE Iowa	Harrison, Pratt, Parsons	1:79
13.1	Plain	4458	AR 15061	1874	Cook farm	Gass	1:117–143
13.2	Plain	8360	AR 15027	1886	SE Iowa	Harrison	5:43–44
13.3	Plain	4461	AR 15064	1874	Cook farm	Gass	1:121
13.4	Plain	4491	AR 15060	1874	Cook farm	Gass	1:117–143
13.5	Plain	4466	AR 15058	1874	Cook farm	Gass	1:122
13.6	Plain	2927	AR 14388	1914	SE Iowa	Michelson	—
13.7	Blank	4559	AR 15024	1875	SE Iowa	Parsons	1:111
14.1	Plain	8359	AR 15028	1886	SE Iowa	Harrison	5:39
14.2	Plain	9656	AR 15016	1908	Ill.	Nickerson	—
14.3	Plain	7066	AR 15059	1880	Ill.	Gass[b]	4:18(?)
14.4	Plain	7620	AR 14382	1881(?)	Ill.	Gass	3:187(?)
14.5	Plain	7623	AR 15062	—	Ill.	—	—
14.6	Plain	4565	AR 15057	1875	SE Iowa	Tiffany	1:113

[a]Genuineness not certain [McKusick].
[b]Collector not excavator.

Finders and Collectors

Tables 1-3 indicate the finders or collectors of the various curved-base platform pipes. The information is taken from the Davenport Academy catalogue records, and there are a few discrepancies and gaps in the records and contradictions with the publications. The listing is a compromise in some cases. Table 4 summarizes the collection of 66 platform pipes by individuals associated with the specimens.

The Gass family was responsible for at least 30 of the 35 fraudulent pipes. Edwin Gass, Jacob's brother, gave no genuine pipes and 15 frauds. Sometimes he "found" them, and on one occasion was at an excavation with Gass when the latter dug one up. Six pipes came from Muscatine, and the remainder are from Rock Island and Mercer Counties in Illinois. Blumer, Jacob Gass' brother-in-law, gave the elephant and was at the same excavation when Gass found a similarly constructed fragmentary bird pipe of grease soaked limestone. Both pipes are here attributed to Blumer. The implication, which I have been unable to confirm, is that Gass' brother and brother-in-law were playing a joke on him. Neither of them was a member of the Academy and bibliographic information is scanty. Small wonder he later complained about being "the victim of all." (Gass 1886MS).

Jacob Gass, himself, gave 14 genuine pipes and was the agency by which other genuine specimens were obtained through purchase or arranging for excavation with Academy funds. The fraudulent pipes, 13 in number, came from purchases with museum funds, or a few from his excavations including those previously visited by the omnipresent janitor, Graham.

Field parties or Academy members gave 16 genuine pipes and no frauds. Persons associated with these donations include those outraged by the charges of Lindley and Tiffany; the donors were French, Harrison, Pratt, Hall, and others. Tiffany himself was associated with at least two genuine specimens, and Lindley was along on several field parties. One can see from this tabulation (table 4) why so many of the Academy members considered the statements by Lindley and Tiffany to be slanders, not to be regarded seriously.

The dates are of interest. The early work by Gass produced all genuine pipes, and no fraudulent pipes came from the Cook Farm. The first elephant, from Louisa County, dates from 1878, a year after the first fraudulent tablets, and the frauds continued at an accelerating rate climaxed by the 15 frauds donated by Edwin Gass in the spring of 1883 when the Gass family left Davenport. This donation was described in PDANS 4:222, 233 and also in *Science* 1:205.

After this donation, no more fraudulent pipes were added to the collection. The unsuccessful search for more elephants continued. Paarman, a curator who succeeded Pratt, excavated a number of mounds. Later, the Academy made its peace with the Smithsonian and supported the excavations of Dr. Truman Michelson, receiving several genuine pipes for its collection in 1914.

Table 4

Excavator or Collector of Pipe Specimens

Excavator or Collector	Genuine Pipes	Fraudulent Pipes
Jacob Gass	14	13
Adolf Blumer	0	2
Edwin Gass	0	15
Academy members and field parties	16	0
Miscellaneous gifts	0	2
No information	1	3
Total	31	35

Material and Craftsmanship

As Shetrone pointed out in his manuscript, the fraudulent pipes are usually made from the wrong material, and the platforms are crude, with rounded edges, and lack the graceful proportions and balance of the genuine specimens.

Material is listed in table 5, which provides a striking contrast between the genuine and spurious artifacts. The genuine pipestone is described by Shetrone as "familiar greenish-drab flinty fire clay, ordinarily known as 'pipestone.' This material, which is readily and positively identifiable, was the favorite material of the Hopewellians throughout the area of their occurrence, and probably was used in the manufacture of 95 per cent of all known pipes from their Tumuli. . . . The flinty fireclay occurs definitely in Scioto County, Ohio, where ancient quarries exist, and doubtless in numerous other localities in the Middle West." (Shetrone 1930MSa). I know of no quarries in Iowa; the genuine specimens were all imported, either as blanks or as finished pipes. The material contrasts strongly with the material of the spurious pipes represented by red ferruginous shale, clay, limestone, and other convenient materials close at hand. The discussion of Iowa pipes contained in the massive survey by George A. West (1934 Part I: 287-289) is based on personal communication by Charles R. Keyes and is both incomplete and inaccurate.

Patination or weathering is present on many of the genuine specimens but not on all of them. Some were cleaned. No true weathering is present on any of the spurious specimens. Shetrone, during this examination, removed various kinds of film or finish used to hide the marks of recent manufacture no longer visible on the specimens.

Table 5
Pipe Material and Platform Size

	Fraudulent				Genuine		
		Platform				Platform	
Plate	Material	Width	Length	Plate	Material	Width	Length
5.1	Limestone	15/16	3 2/16	11.1	Green pipestone	1 7/16	3 6/16
5.2	Limestone	1	4 7/16	11.2	Green pipestone	1 3/16	3 1/16
5.3	Argillite or			11.3	Green pipestone	1 3/16	3 5/16
	slate(?)	1 4/16	3 2/16	12.1	Green pipestone	1 6/16	3 7/16
6.1	Sandstone	1	3 10/16	12.3	Green pipestone	1 7/16	3 4/16
6.2	Limestone	1	—	12.5	Red and green		
6.3	Clay(?)	1 2/16	3 7/16		pipestone	1 5/16	3 6/16
7.1	Limestone	1 2/16	3 9/16	13.1	Calcite	1 2/16	2 3/16
7.2	Limestone	1	3	13.2	Green pipestone	1 1/16	2 8/16
7.3	Limestone	1 4/16	3 14/16	13.3	Green pipestone	1 2/16	2 11/16
8.1	Talc	1 4/16	4	13.4	Green pipestone	1 1/16	2 8/16
8.2	Talc(?)	1 1/16	4 1/16	13.5	Green pipestone	1 4/16	2 11/16
8.3	Clay(?)	1 3/16	2 10/16	13.6	Gray pipestone	1 3/16	3 2/16(est.)
9.1	Talc	1 14/16	3 3/16	13.7	Welded tuff	1 8/16	3 4/16
9.2	Red catlinite	11/16	3 11/16	14.1	Calcite	1 9/16	3 2/16
9.3	Limestone	15/16	3 5/16	14.2	Green pipestone	1 3/16	3
9.4	Limestone	1	2 13/16	14.3	Green pipestone	1 5/16	2 14/16
9.5	Limestone	1 5/16	—	14.4	Green pipestone	1 3/16	3 3/16
10.1	Clay(?)	13/16	2 3/16	14.5	Green pipestone	1 3/16	3 5/16
10.2	Clay(?)	11/16	2 5/16	14.6	Red pipestone	1 3/16	4 1/16
10.3	Red slate	1	3 5/16				
10.4	Red slate	1	2 3/16				
10.5	Red slate	1 1/16	2 7/16				
10.6	Red slate	1	—				
10.7	Clay(?)	1 1/16	3 1/16				
10.8	Clay(?)	9/16	2 5/16				

Width and length measured in inches and fractions. No significant differences occur between spurious and genuine pipes.

Shoe blacking covered fresh stone on the so-called howling wolf pipe (plate 8.1) and a plain bowl specimen (7388) now missing. A thick black gummy substance, which had partially peeled off upon drying exposing fresh stone, had covered the lizard pipe (plate 8.2). A metallic coating, possibly from a lead pencil, covered the missing lizard pipe (7619).

Oil or grease was used to give an appearance of age on six specimens. Fraudulent specimens so treated were the two elephants (plate 5.1, 2), a broken bird effigy (plate 6.2), and an animal variously termed a seal or otter but which may be a beaver (plate 7.2). Two missing specimens similarly treated were a swan effigy (7061) and a plain platform pipe (7067).

An unknown paste substance, which washed or brushed off, covered fresh incisions on the swan pipe (plate 6.1) and a plain pipe now missing from the collection (8357).

Fire was used to mask freshly prepared surfaces on six other specimens, all but the turtle, for which information is lacking, being donations of Edwin Gass. The turtle (plate 8.3) also was treated with glue. The remainder of burned specimens were two other amorphous animals (plates 6.3 and 10.8) and three plain platform pipes (plate 10.1, 2, 7).

Four other fraudulent specimens were apparently carved with a jackknife from a ferruginous red shale, almost a hematite. No effort was made to conceal the fresh incisions. Two of these were excavated by Jacob Gass, one was given by his brother Edwin, and there are no data on one of them. One is an animal and the remainder are plain (plate 10.3, 4, 5, 6).

In summary, 12 of the 34 fraudulent artifacts were treated with grease, gum, lead pencil, shoe blacking, or some other substance to hide freshly worked surfaces. Six others were burned for the same purpose. At least four more still bore marks of the jackknife used in making them. The remaining 12 had little or no surface treatment to mask the recent fabrication.

Three Indices

Although a number of different indices could be applied to illustrate the differences between the genuine and spurious pipes, I am limiting the discussion to three measurements based upon my restudy of the collection.

Pipe Stem Hole Diameter. A series of drill bits was compared with the pipe stem holes, the match being made with the butt or smooth end fitting snugly when pushed through the opening in the bowl. The distribution of hole sizes is presented in table 6. It appears that a 3/32 inch drill bit would account for most of the fraudulent specimens, particularly if one adds the five specimens of the next larger size as might be accountable by drill wear enlarging the hole. The genuine specimens tend to have larger holes, as can be seen in the distribution.

Pipe Bowl Hole Angle. A common feature of the genuine specimens is a bowl hole vertical to the platform. Among the frauds, the bowl sometimes slopes slightly towards the front of the pipe, forming an oblique angle. The distribution of vertical versus oblique bowls is presented in table 7.

Only one of the specimens classed as genuine has a slightly oblique bowl hole. The remainder are vertical, and none is indeterminate. Among the fabrications, vertical bowls are much less common and many are offset. The large group of indeterminates results from extremely shallow bowls on some of the most obviously recent and crudely made specimens.

Platform Length-Width Index. When some of the less sophisticated amateurs made pipes, they conceived of them as they were illustrated, usually in side profile. In consequence they tended to underestimate platform width. The formula

$$\frac{\text{Maximum Width x } 100}{\text{Maximum Length}} = \text{Width Index}$$

provides a striking separation of the two groups (table 8). The single specimen of the "genuine" group falling within the 2.6-3.0 range is number 4565 (plate 14.6), having an index of 2.9. It appears genuine on all other characteristics but has an unusually large bowl.

The various lines of evidence considered in this appendix substantiate the documentary sources of the archaeological frauds carried out at or near the Academy during the years from 1877 to early spring 1883. Although Lindley insisted that specimens were still being made in the basement for almost two more years, until January 1885, none of these later ones was put in the excavations or appeared in the collections donated to the Academy.

Table 6

Minimum Pipe Stem Hole Diameters

Diameter (1/64 inches)	Genuine		Spurious	
	Number	%	Number	%
10	0	—	0	—
9	1	5.5	0	—
8	6	33	1	4
7	6	33	5	22
6	4	22	13	56
5	0	—	3	13
4	1	5.5	1	4
3	0	—	0	—

Table 7

Comparison of Oblique *versus* Vertical Bowl Holes

Bowl	Genuine		Spurious	
	Number	%	Number	%
Oblique	1	5	11	44
Vertical	18	95	5	20
Indeterminate	—	—	9	36

Table 8

Length-Width Index

Index Ranges	Genuine		Spurious	
	Number	%	Number	%
1.5-2.0	0	—	1	4
2.1-2.5	0	—	3	12
2.6-3.0	1	5	7	31
3.1-3.5	0	—	7	31
3.6-4.0	8	42	1	4
4.1-4.5	6	32	3	12
4.6-5.0	4	21	0	—
5.1-5.5	0	—	0	—
5.6-6.0	0	—	1	4

Bibliography

References included in the bibliography are limited to publications and manuscripts cited in the text, with the addition of papers written by the principals concerned in various ways with the Davenport frauds, permitting a somewhat fuller evaluation of their work. For example, A. S. Tiffany published a paper entitled "Report on the Results of an Excursion to Albany, Illinois, Nov. 7th and 8th, 1873." Not directly cited, the title conveys a vivid impression of his limited scientific orientation to archaeological research.

Manuscripts are included by author under a separate listing. All documents cited are available in photocopy in the Special Collections, The University of Iowa Library. Cooperation by the Davenport Museum in permitting these copies to be made is acknowledged with appreciation. All originals of manuscripts are at the Davenport Museum unless otherwise noted.

The abbreviation *PDANS* is the *Proceedings of the Davenport Academy of Natural Sciences; AA* is the *American Antiquarian and Oriental Journal; Am. Nat.* is the *American Naturalist; AAAS* is the *American Association for the Advancement of Science;* and *Ann. Rept. USBE* designates the *Annual Reports of the United States Bureau of Ethnology.* The published *Proceedings* of the Davenport Academy have proven to be invaluable because they record the meetings and summarize the content of discussions about the case. In some instances where author attribution is unclear, the relevant volume and page is cited directly in the text. Volumes in Roman numerals appear in Arabic numeral equivalents.

Publications

Allen, W. R.
    1893 President's Annual Address. *PDANS* 5:316-319.
    1894 President's Annual Address. *PDANS* 6:328-330.

Bailey, John
    1948 An Unsolved Davenport Mystery. *Contemporary Club Papers* 52:1-19. Davenport.

Barber, Edwin A.
    1882 Mound Pipes. *Am. Nat.* 16:265-280.

Barris, W. H.
    1893 A Defense of Our Local Geology. *PDANS* 5:15-22. [Read 1886].

Berlin, A. F.
    1886 Fraudulent Objects of Stone. *AA* 8:97-101. [Correspondence].
    1886a Fraudulent Stone Objects, and the Gass Correspondence. *AA* 8:228-230.

Blumer, Rev. A.
    1882 Exploration of Mounds in Louisa County, Iowa. *PDANS* 3:132-133. [submitted 1880].

Calvin, Samuel
    1893 Prehistoric Iowa. In *Iowa Historical Lectures.* pp. 5-29. Iowa City: Iowa State Historical Society. [Delivered Dec. 1891].

Campbell, John
    1882 Proposed Reading of the Davenport Tablets. *AA* 4:145-153.
    1883 The Mound Builders Identified. *Proc. AAAS* 32:419-421. [abstract].

Christensen, Thomas P.
    1952   The Mound Builders. *Annals of Iowa* 3rd ser. 31:300-308.
Farquharson, R. J.
    1875   Recent Explorations of Mounds near Davenport, Iowa. *AAAS Trans.*
           18:297-315.
    1876   Recent Archaeological Discoveries at Davenport, Iowa, of Copper
           Axes, Cloth, etc., Supposed to have come down to us from a Pre-
           Historic People, called the Mound-Builders. *PDANS* 1:117-143.
    1877   On the Inscribed Tablets, found by Rev. J. Gass in a Mound near
           Davenport, Iowa. *PDANS* 2:103-116.
    1877a The Davenport Tablets. *Proceedings of the American Antiquarian So-
           ciety* 69:64-69. Worcester, Mass.
    1879   [Concerning Davenport Tablets] Correspondence. *AA* 1:167-168.
    1880   The Elephant Pipe. *AA* 2:67-69.
Gass, Jacob
    1877   [Note of a communication describing the stone tablets from Cook
           Farm Mound]. *PDANS* 2:81-82.
    1877a A Connected Account of the Explorations of Mound 3, Cook's Farm
           Group. *PDANS* 2:92-98.
    1877b Report of Exploration of Mound No. 10, Cook's Farm Group. *PDANS*
           2:141-142.
    1877c Description of Some Inscribed Stones found in Cleona Township,
           Scott County, Iowa. *PDANS* 2:142.
    1878   Examination of a Large Mound in Jackson County, Iowa. *PDANS*
           2:155.
    1880   Inscribed Rocks in Cleona Township. *PDANS* 2:172-173.
    1880a Report on a Mound in Jackson County. *PDANS* 2:173.
    1880b Mound Explorations in Jackson County, Iowa. *PDANS* 2:219-220.
    1880c Report of Exploration of Indian Graves. *PDANS* 2:291-293.
    1880d Explorations of Six Indian Burial Grounds in the Vicinity of the
           Mouth of the Rock River. *PDANS* 2:354-355.
    1882   Report of Exploration of Mounds in Rock Island County, Ill., in 1879
           and 1880. *PDANS* 3:135-139.
    1882a Exploration of Mounds in Louisa County, Iowa. *PDANS* 3:140-146.
    1882b Exploration of Mounds in Mercer County, Ill. *PDANS* 3:147-148.
    1882c Ancient Fortification in Louisa County, Iowa. *PDANS* 3:183-184.
    1882d Mound Exploration in 1881. *PDANS* 3:186-193.
Gass, Jacob and R. J. Farquharson
    1880   Explorations of a Mound near Moline, Ill. *PDANS* 2:289-290.
Griffin, J. B.
    1965   Review of *Men of Ancient Iowa. Wisconsin Archaeologist* 46:157-165.
Gurney, O. R.
    1952   *The Hittites.* Harmondsworth, Middlesex: Penguin/Pelican.
Harrison, Charles E.
    1880   Exploration of Mound No. 11, Cook's Farm Group, and Discovery of
           an Inscribed Tablet of Limestone. *PDANS* 2:221-224.
    1886   Report of Mound Exploration Near Pine Creek, Muscatine County,
           Iowa. *PDANS* 4:197-198.

Harrison, Charles E. and W. H. Pratt
    1893   Additional Explorations at Toolesboro. *PDANS* 5:43-44.
Haven, Samuel F.
    1855   Archaeology of the United States . . . *Proceedings of the American Antiquarian Society* vol. 25. Worcester, Mass.
Henshaw, Henry W.
    1883   Animal Carvings from Mounds of the Mississippi Valley. *Second Ann. Rept. USBE* pp. 117-166.
Hrdlicka, Ales
    1907   Skeletal Remains Suggesting or Attributed to Early Man in North America. *Bulletin Bur. Am. Ethnol.* no. 33.
Jennings, Jesse D.
    1968   *Prehistory of North America*. New York: McGraw-Hill.
Keyes, Charles R.
    1920   Some Materials for the Study of Iowa Archaeology. *Iowa Journal of History and Politics* 18:357-370.
Lindley, Clarence
    1876   Mound Explorations in 1875. *PDANS* 1:111-113.
    1877   Mound Explorations in Jackson County, Iowa. *PDANS* 2:83-84.
Lynch, E. P., H. C. Fulton, C. E. Harrison, and C. H. Preston
    1893   Mound Explorations at Toolesboro, Louisa County, Iowa. *PDANS* 5:37-44.
Mason, Otis T.
    1878   Anthropological News. *Am. Nat.* 12:322-323.
    1878a   "The Davenport Tablet" in General Notes, Anthropology. *Am. Nat.* 12:400.
    1880   "Mound Builders" in General Notes, Anthropology. *Am. Nat.* 14:216-217.
    1880a   "Another Elephant Pipe" in General Notes, Anthropology. *Am. Nat.* 14:455.
    1880b   "The Davenport Academy" in General Notes, Anthropology. *Am. Nat.* 14:814-815.
    1884   [Review of Henshaw in] General Notes, Anthropology. *Am. Nat.* 18:953-954.
    1886   "The Davenport Academy" in General Notes, Anthropology. *Am. Nat.* 20:671-673.
McKusick, Marshall
    1964   *Men of Ancient Iowa: As Revealed by Archaeological Discoveries.* Ames, Iowa: Iowa State University Press.
Murdock, Samuel
    1888   Prehistoric Races. *Iowa Historical Record* 4: 28-32.
Peet, Stephen D.
    1879   Recent Mound Explorations. *AA* 1:109.
    1880   Report of Discovery of Elephant Pipe no. 2. *AA* 2:320.
    1884   Mound Explorations in Iowa. *AA* 6:276.
    1886   Are the Davenport Tablets Frauds? *AA* 8: 46-56.
    1886a   The Points Involved. *AA* 8:117-119.
    1886b   "Pipes and Mounds" in Archaeological Notes. *AA* 8:256.

1886c Extra-Limital Animals and Mound Builder's Pipes. *AA* 8:308-313.
1887   The Mastodon in America and the Mound Builders. *AA* 9:242-247.
1887a "Elephant Pipes." *AA* 9:250-251.
1891   The Mysterious Race. *AA* 13:266-275.
1892   The Mound-Builders and the Mastodon. *AA* 14:59-86.
1903   *The Mound Builders: their Works and Relics.* 2nd ed. Chicago: American Antiquarian.

Petersen, William J.
1951   Charles Reuben Keyes. *The Palimpsest* 32:281-284.

Powell, Major J. W.
1883   Report of the Director. *Second Ann. Rept. USBE* xxx-xxxiii. [Henshaw's report].
1890   Prehistoric Man in America. *The Forum* 8:489-503.
1894   Report of the Director. *Twelfth Ann. Rept. USBE* xxix-xlvii. [Thomas' report].

Pratt, W. H.
1876   Report of Exploration of the Ancient Mounds of Albany, Whiteside County, Illinois. *PDANS* 1:99-104.
1876a Report of Explorations of the Ancient Mounds at Toolesboro, Louisa County, Iowa. *PDANS* 1:106-111.
1877   Shell Money and Other Primitive Currencies. *PDANS* 2:38-46.
1880   On the Exploration of the Mounds on the Farm of Col. Wm. Allen. *PDANS* 2:148-150, 154.
1880a Reminiscences of the Early History of the Academy. *PDANS* 2:193-202.
1880b Curious Relic from the Cook Farm. *PDANS* 2:256-257.
1882   Inscribed Rock at Sterling, Ill. *PDANS* 3:89-90.
1882a Exploration of a Mound on the Allen Farm. *PDANS* 3:90-91.
1882b The President's Annual Address. *PDANS* 3:151-157.
1886   The Davenport Tablets Genuine. *AA* 8:92-96.

Preston, C. H.
1886   Mound Exploration near Joslyn, Rock Island County, Illinois. *PDANS* 4:198-200.

Putnam, Charles E.
1885   Elephant Pipes and Inscribed Tablets in the Museum of the Academy of Natural Sciences, Davenport. [1st edition].
1886   Elephant Pipes and Inscribed Tablets in the Museum of the Academy of Natural Sciences, Davenport. *PDANS* 4 (appendix):251-348. [Reprint of 1885 pamphlet with correspondence added].
1886a The Davenport Tablets. *Science* 7, no. 157:119-120.
1886b The Davenport Tablets. *Science* 7, no. 171:437-439.

Rust, H. N.
1882   The Davenport Tablets [abstract]. *Proc. AAAS* 31:584-585.

Schwartz, Douglas W.
1967   *Conceptions of Kentucky Prehistory.* Lexington: University of Kentucky Press. Studies in Anthropology, no. 6.

Seyffarth, G.
1882   The Indian Inscriptions of Davenport, Iowa. *PDANS* 3:72-80.

Silverberg, Robert
    1968   *Mound Builders of Ancient America: the Archaeology of a Myth.*
           Greenwich, Connecticut: New York Graphic Society.
Squier, E. G., and E. H. Davis
    1848   Ancient Monuments of the Mississippi Valley: Comprising the Results
           of Extensive Original Surveys and Exploration. *Smithsonian Institution
           Contributions to Knowledge,* vol. 1.
Starr, Frederick
    1897   Bibliography of Iowa Antiquities *and* Summary of the Archaeology of
           Iowa. *PDANS* 6:1-24, and 53-124. [Note: issued as separate items
           dated 1892 and 1895 respectively.]
    1897a The Davenport Academy of Natural Sciences. *Popular Science Month-
           ly.* 51:83-98.
    1897b Circular of Suggestions Regarding Work in Archaeology. *PDANS*
           6:340-343.
Thomas, Cyrus
    1885   The Davenport Tablet. *Science* 6, no. 151:564.
    1886   The Davenport Tablet. *Science* 7, no. 152:10-11.
    1886a The Davenport Tablets. *Science* 7, no. 152:189-190.
    1894   Report on Mound Explorations of the Bureau of Ethnology. *Twelfth
           Ann. Rept. USBE* pp. 1-730.
Thompson, James
    1892   President's Annual Address. *PDANS* 6:304-307.
Tiffany, A. S.
    1876   Discovery of Human Remains in a Shell-bed on Rock Island. *PDANS*
           1:42-43.
    1876a An Ancient Copper Implement Donated by E. B. Baldwin. *PDANS*
           1:59.
    1876b Pre-historic Cremation Furnace. *PDANS* 1:64-65.
    1876c Report on the Results of the Excursion to Albany, Illinois, Nov. 7th
           and 8th, 1873. *PDANS* 1:104-106.
    1876d Mound Explorations in 1875. *PDANS* 1:113-114.
Uhle, Max
    1886   Zwei prähistorische Elephantendarstellungen aus Amerika. *Zeitschrift
           für Ethnologie* 18:322-328.
Wahlgren, Erik
    1958   *The Kensington Stone, a Mystery Solved.* Madison: University of
           Wisconsin Press.
Ward, Duren
    1903   Anthropological Instruction in Iowa. *Iowa Journal of History and
           Politics* 3:3-23.
Watson, Warren
    1890   Those Elephant Pipes Again. *The Naturalist* vol. 4, no. 7 [Unpagi-
           nated publication].
Wauchope, Robert
    1962   *Lost Tribes and Sunken Continents: Myth and Method in the Study
           of American Indians.* Chicago: University of Chicago Press.
Weiner, J. S.
    1955   *The Piltdown Forgery.* Oxford: Oxford University Press.

West, George A.
>   1934   Tobacco, Pipes and Smoking Customs of the American Indians. *Bulletin, Milwaukee Public Museum* vol. 17: parts I and II.

Willey, Gordon R.
>   1966   *An Introduction to American Archaeology* vol. 1, *North and Middle America*. New York: Prentice-Hall.

Manuscripts

Anonymous
>   1886MS   Note to Putnam alleging collusion between S. D. Peet and Major J. W. Powell in rejecting the Davenport relics. Postmarked 22 January 1886, Washington, D.C. Signed "A Friend of Justice."

Baird, Spencer
>   1877MS   Letter dated 26 June to J. Duncan Putnam, on Smithsonian National Museum letterhead, which rejects E. Foreman's Report on the Davenport tablets.

Berlin, A. F.
>   1886MS   Letter to C. E. Putnam from Allentown, Pennsylvania, dated 9 January, quoting a letter Berlin has received from Cyrus Thomas, Bureau of Ethnology, on the fraudulent nature of the relics J. Gass traded to H. C. Stevens.

>   1886MSa   Letter to C. E. Putnam from Allentown, Pennsylvania, dated 28 January, quoting an affidavit received from H. C. Stevens.

Claypole, E. W.
>   1886MS   Letter to W. H. Pratt from Akron, Ohio, dated 6 February, discussing a geological fraud at the Davenport Academy.

Foreman, E.
>   1877MS   Correspondence to J. Duncan Putnam from the National Museum, Smithsonian, dated 14 May and 22 June, in which Foreman rejects the authenticity of the Davenport tablets.

>   1877MSa   "Report on Three Inscribed Slate Tablets from a Mound near Davenport, Iowa." Handwritten nine-page report on legal size paper, headed in script "National Museum."

Gass, Erbe
>   1969MS   Transcript of interview in Postville, Iowa, with Arthur Gass and Hertha Gass Erbe, son and daughter of the Reverend Jacob Gass. Recorded by J. N. Young, it concerns Gass' knowledge of the frauds. (Original, The University of Iowa).

Gass, Jacob
>   1886MS   Letter to W. H. Pratt, dated 13 April, Postville, Iowa. German original not present. This copy is an English translation and not in Gass' handwriting, in which he admits to being "the victim of all."

Harrison, C. E.
>   1886MS   Report to Fulton and the investigating committee relative to Tiffany's conduct, dated 2 January. Handwritten, two and one-half pages, legal size paper.

Hurlbut, Irving
    1969MS Judge James Bollinger's narrative told to Hurlbut and John Bailey in the 1940s concerning tablet and pipe frauds. Retold to Mc-Kusick and J. N. Young at Muscatine, 23 March. (Original, The University of Iowa).
    1969MSa Correspondence addressed to McKusick relative to the Bollinger narrative. (Originals, The University of Iowa).

Jones, William
    1886MS Letter to Putnam and Rogers, Attorneys, dated 12 April, Clinton, Wisconsin. It concerns a prospective libel suit against S. D. Peet.

Latourette, C. D. and D. C. Latourette
    1886MS Letter to C. E. Putnam from Oregon City, Oregon, dated 19 March, in which they agree to act in a libel suit against H. C. Stevens if there is a good case.

Lindley, Clarence T.
    1886MS Statement that Lindley had personally seen platform pipes made in the Academy building during the period from 1 January 1880 through 1 January 1885. Sworn and notarized by L. M. Fisher, Notary Public, Scott County, with seal.

Mason, Otis T.
    1886MS Letter to C. E. Putnam dated 1 May, on National Museum letter-head concerning his reluctance to becoming embroiled in the Davenport controversy.

McCowen, Jennie
    1886MS Minutes of the 26 March General Meeting of the Academy concerned with the expulsion of A. S. Tiffany. Handwritten. In photocopy it covers eleven pages of legal size paper. Originally transcribed on both sides of two extremely long sheets.
    1886MSa Minutes of the 28 May General Meeting of the Academy concerned with the expulsion of C. T. Lindley. Handwritten and typed versions. Originally misdated 28 June, typed copies undated. Apparently taken down by a professional secretary since Lindley had protested inaccuracies in the earlier March minutes, this handwritten copy was corrected by McCowen, and is sixteen pages in length. (There is a second version, typed without original, having many inaccuracies, which cannot be attributed to McCowen. It emphasizes Lindley's guilt in making fraudulent relics.)
    1886MSb Notes taken of Lindley's testimony at two meetings.

Peet, S. D.
    1886MS Letter to C. E. Putnam from Clinton, Wisconsin, dated 27 April, in which Peet bitterly complains about Putnam's threatened libel suit and general troublemaking. Peet states he will publish the Gass defense if it is actually written by Gass himself.

Phelps, J. B.
    1886MS Minutes of the committee investigating the conduct of C. T. Lindley. It contains hearings and testimony with reports and correspondence by Mr. and Mrs. Graham, Lindley, Preston, Pratt, Putnam, and Sheldon. The questioning by Lindley of the Grahams

concerning pipe manufacture and Pratt's behavior, together with a full statement of Lindley's charges, makes this manuscript group a key part of the collection.

Pratt, W. H.

1886MS Report to H. C. Fulton, chairman of the special committee investigating the conduct of A. S. Tiffany. Pratt replies to various verbal and written statements made by Tiffany about the fraudulent nature of the tablets and elephant pipes, reporting the charges are without foundation. Dated January.

1886MSa Report to the special committee investigating A. S. Tiffany. It concerns Tiffany's conflicts over Academy policy. Unsigned, undated, in Pratt's handwriting; probably dates from January 1886.

1887-   Notes to Putnam regarding the men on the opposition ticket, and
1889MS   a lengthy report on Lindley's activities during the period of his membership. He accuses Lindley of fraud in attempting to obtain compensation for his collection damaged in a state building. He also accuses Lindley of accepting specimens on behalf of the Academy and then putting them in his personal collection.

Preston, C. H.

1885-   Secretary of special committee investigating A. S. Tiffany. Minutes
1886MS   of the meetings from 30 December to 4 March, including the testimony of Dr. C. T. Lindley. Handwritten, five and one-half pages, legal size paper.

Putnam, C. E.

1885MS Copy of telegram to S. D. Peet dated 19 December accusing him of "miserable libel."

1886MS Typed copy of letter to S. D. Peet dated 20 April, in which he argues that Gass' defense must be routed through the Academy rather than being sent off directly to Peet by Gass.

1887MS Letter to W. H. Pratt dated 31 January, requesting detailed information on the men who formed "an opposition" group to his leadership within the Academy.

1887MSa Letter to the editor of the *Davenport Democrat* countering the published newspaper story in the *Rock Island Argus* about the factional fighting at the Academy. Eight typescript pages, the article is dated 5 February. (Note: a number of other manuscripts by Putnam are in the files but are not enumerated here.)

Rock Island Argus

1887   Newspaper story, unsigned, headlined "The Factional Fight." It is subtitled "The Academy of Science at Davenport—The Election—Cause of the Trouble—All's Well That Ends Well." Dated 27 January.

Schroeder, Stan

1969MS Excerpts from the newspaper, the *Postville Herald,* describing the career of Jacob Gass in the 1890s (Original, The University of Iowa).

Shetrone, Henry C.

1930MS Report to E. K. Putnam "The Davenport Elephant Pipes and Inscribed Tablets."

1930MSa "Memoranda on the Davenport Public Museum Pipes to be used in formulating a report."

1930MSb Catalogue notes.

Tiffany, A. S.

1882MS Letter to P. W. Norris, Bureau of Ethnology, dated 27 October, in which he states the limestone tablet is a fraud and implicates C. E. Harrison. He further adds that the elephant pipes were frauds and "planted" on J. Gass.

1886MS A statement prepared in his defense and presented to the committee investigating his conduct. Typescript, seven pages, legal size paper.

Thomas, Cyrus

1885MS Letter to C. E. Putnam dated 5 December from the Bureau of Ethnology. Thomas refuses to send a copy of Tiffany's 1882 letter to anyone but Tiffany himself.

Wright, R. E. Sons

1886MS Letter dated 15 March to C. E. Putnam from R. E. Wright's Sons, Attorneys, Allentown, Pennsylvania, relative to a possible libel suit against A. F. Berlin.

Young, J. N.

1969MS Notes and worksheets on the pipes in the Davenport Museum.

Plates

Plate 1.   Cremation Scene Tablet

Plate 2.   Hunting Scene Tablet

Plate 3.   Calendar Stone Tablet

Plate 4.   Limestone Tablet

Plate 5.   Elephant and Bear Platform Pipe Frauds

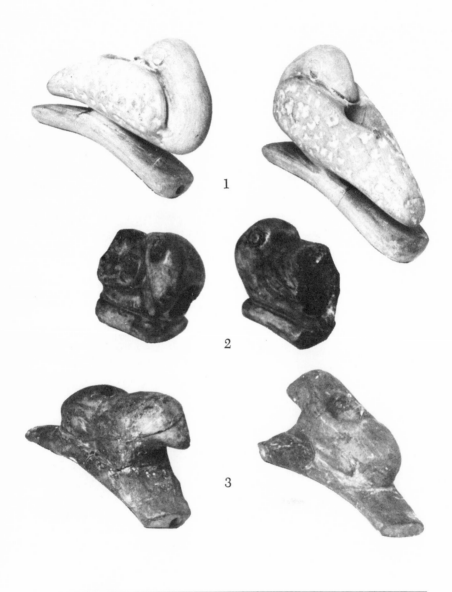

Plate 6.   Bird and Animal Platform Pipe Frauds

Plate 7.   Human and Animal Platform Pipe Frauds

Plate 8.   Animal Platform Pipe Frauds

Plate 9.   Bird and Animal Platform Pipe Frauds

Plate 10.   Plain and Animal Platform Pipe Frauds

Plate 11.   "Genuine" Effigy Platform Pipes

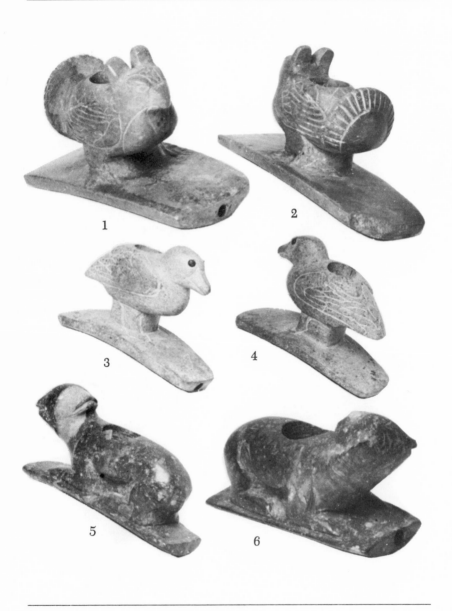

Plate 12.   "Genuine" Effigy Platform Pipes

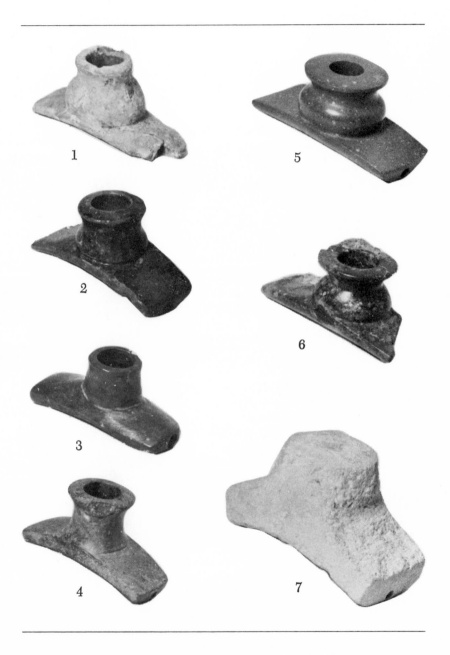

Plate 13.   "Genuine" Plain Platform Pipes

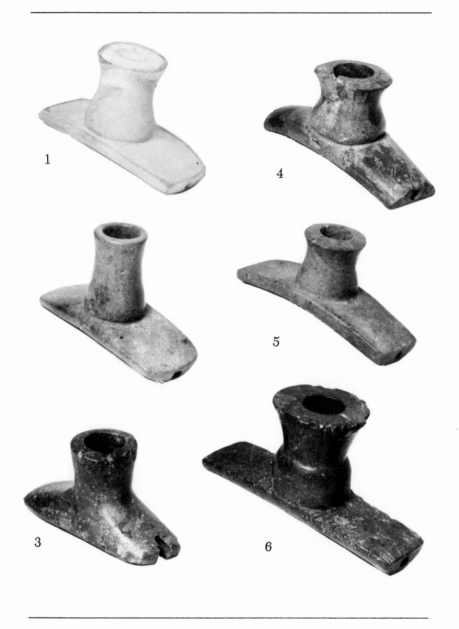

Plate 14.   "Genuine" Plain Platform Pipes

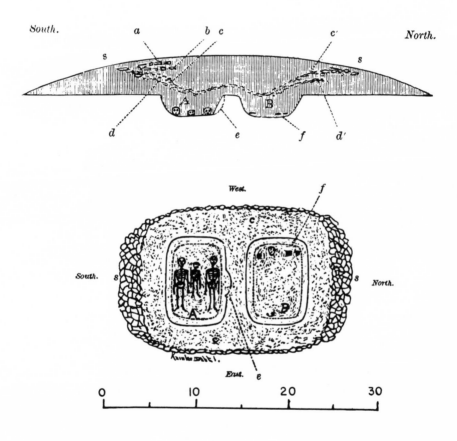

Plate 15.   Plan of Cook Farm Mound 3: *A* undisturbed pit. *B* disturbed burial pit where tablets were found

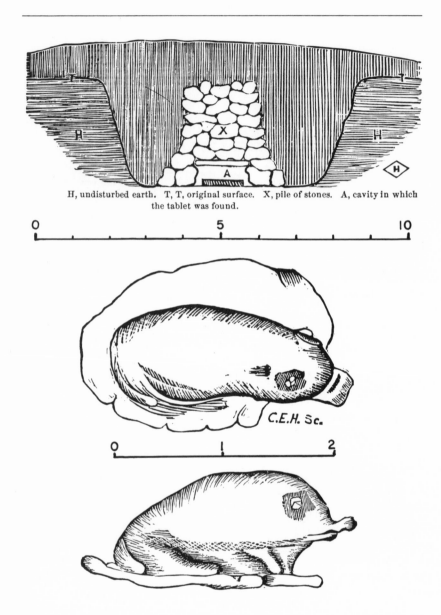

H, undisturbed earth.   T, T, original surface.   X, pile of stones.   A, cavity in which
the tablet was found.

Plate 16.   Plan of Cook Farm Mound 11: A cavity where limestone
tablet was found. Concretion from Mound 3

R. J. Farquharson

Charles E. Putnam

W. H. Pratt

W. H. Barris

Plate 17. Four Presidents of the Davenport Academy during the Controversy

Plate 18.   The Davenport Academy and Pipes Made by the Janitor
in its Basement

Plate 19. Judge Bollinger and his Shingle from the Old Slate House

Plate 20.   The Reverend Jacob Gass

Plate 21.   Mr. A. S. Tiffany

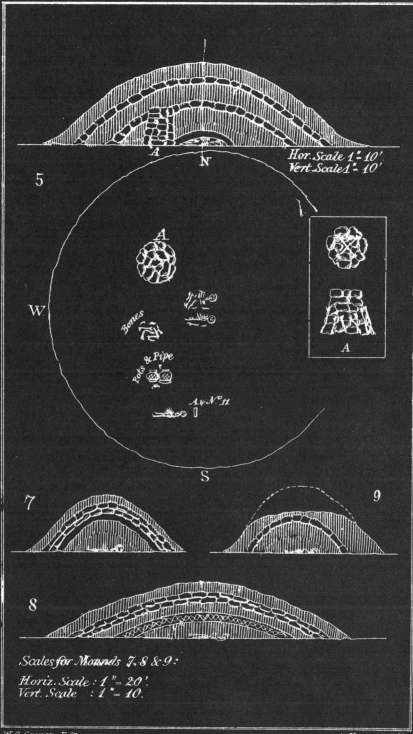